New Directions for
Student Services

John H. Schuh
EDITOR-IN-CHIEF

Elizabeth J. Whitt
ASSOCIATE EDITOR

Intersections of Religious Privilege: Difficult Dialogues and Student Affairs Practice

Sherry K. Watt
Ellen E. Fairchild
Kathleen M. Goodman
EDITORS

Number 125 • Spring 2009
Jossey-Bass
San Francisco

INTERSECTIONS OF RELIGIOUS PRIVILEGE: DIFFICULT DIALOGUES AND
STUDENT AFFAIRS PRACTICE
Sherry K. Watt, Ellen E. Fairchild, Kathleen M. Goodman (eds.)
New Directions for Student Services, no. 125
John H. Schuh, Editor-in-Chief
Elizabeth J. Whitt, Associate Editor

NEW DIRECTIONS FOR STUDENT SERVICES (ISSN 0164-7970, e-ISSN 1536-
0695) is part of The Jossey-Bass Higher and Adult Education Series and
is published quarterly by Wiley Subscription Services, Inc., A Wiley Company, at Jossey-Bass, 989 Market Street, San Francisco, California 94103-
1741. Periodicals Postage Paid at San Francisco, California, and at
additional mailing offices. POSTMASTER: Send address changes to New
Directions for Student Services, Jossey-Bass, 989 Market Street, San Francisco, CA 94103-1741.

New Directions for Student Services is indexed in CIJE: Current Index to
Journals in Education (ERIC), Contents Pages in Education (T&F),
Current Abstracts (EBSCO), Education Index/Abstracts (H.W. Wilson),
Educational Research Abstracts Online (T&F), ERIC Database (Educa-
tion Resources Information Center), and Higher Education Abstracts
(Claremont Graduate University).

Microfilm copies of issues and articles are available in 16mm and 35mm,
as well as microfiche in 105mm, through University Microfilms Inc., 300
North Zeeb Road, Ann Arbor, Michigan 48106-1346.

SUBSCRIPTIONS cost $89 for individuals and $228 for institutions, agencies,
and libraries in the United States. See ordering information page at end
of book.

EDITORIAL CORRESPONDENCE should be sent to the Editor-in-Chief, John
H. Schuh, N 243 Lagomarcino Hall, Iowa State University, Ames, Iowa
50011.

www.josseybass.com

CONTENTS

EDITORS' NOTES

Eight years ago, while introducing an issue of New Directions for Student Services on the topic of student spirituality, Jablonski (2001) stated that the reason for publishing the issue was that "student affairs and student affairs preparation programs have been reluctant to address spirituality . . ." (p. 1). In the intervening years, the topic of spirituality has become ubiquitous in student affairs and higher education. As demonstrated by numerous articles in *About Campus* (for example, Lindholm, 2007), *Liberal Education* (for example, Adler, 2007), and the *Journal of College Student Development* (for example, Love, Bock, Jannarone, and Richardson, 2005). Books have been written on the topic (for example, Chickering, Dalton, and Stamm, 2006), both NASPA and ACPA have dedicated entire conferences to the issue, the Higher Education Research Institute (2004–2005) has undertaken a national longitudinal study of spirituality and college students, and the theme has been approached in student affairs preparation programs (Rogers and Love, 2007). Indeed, student affairs has moved forth with the unquestioned assumption that spirituality is a one-size-fits-all concept for working with students, while the definitions of *religion* and *spirituality* have become conflated and even contested (Goodman and Teraguchi, 2008).

This volume of New Directions for Student Services seeks to further the profession's understanding of spirituality and student affairs practice by focusing on intersections of religious privilege that lead to difficult dialogues. The chapter authors highlight the historic, current, and potential conflicts between those who practice a religion and those who do not, as well as capture the differences between those who are part of a privileged religion versus those who practice in a marginalized religion. In addition to describing the conflicts, the authors share practical suggestions on how to manage difficult dialogues surrounding these topics.

The basic theme behind this volume is inspired by three questions: What inequities exist between the religious and nonreligious, as well as the privileged and marginalized religions? What are the historical and potential conflicts caused by these inequities? And what can student affairs professionals do to cultivate an environment that supports productive dialogue on issues surrounding religious privilege? As informed by Fried (2007) and for the purposes of this volume, religious privilege is a dominant worldview whereby nonsecular values, beliefs, and practices are unconsciously accepted and where secular or nondominant (that is, Islam, Judaism, atheism) belief systems are marginalized.

NEW DIRECTIONS FOR STUDENT SERVICES, no. 125, Spring 2009   © Wiley Periodicals, Inc.
Published online in Wiley InterScience (www.interscience.wiley.com) • DOI: 10.1002/ss.301

We assume that by engaging students, faculty, and staff in these difficult dialogues regarding different aspects of religious privilege, student affairs practitioners will be expanding students' critical thoughts and providing fuel for their search for purpose and meaning in life. Furthermore, we hope that the practical strategies shared here will help student affairs practitioners engage students in dialogue that will move them beyond debates about good and evil on this topic and toward more nuanced understandings and appreciation of difference.

In Chapter One, Ellen E. Fairchild sets the context by describing the historical context of Christian and religious privilege that is important to interactions on campuses today. In Chapter Two, Tricia A. Seifert and Noël Holman-Harmon provide the results of a survey that sheds new light on how student affairs professionals define their spirituality relative to student affairs practices.

Chapters Three through Eight focus on specific student populations. Dafina Lazarus Stewart and Adele Lozano explore the ways that cultural and religious traditions may overlap and intersect in the identities and meaning-making processes of students of color in Chapter Three. In Chapter Four, Warren J. Blumenfeld and Jacqueline R. Klein discuss the challenges Jewish students on campus face. In Chapter Five, Richard W. McCarty provides suggestions for discussions navigating difficult dialogues that intersect the deeply personal nature of religious and sexual identity. In Chapter Six, Saba Rasheed Ali and Elham Bagheri describe Muslim college students and provide suggestions for ways to combat hostility toward Islamic religious groups. In Chapter Seven, Kathleen M. Goodman and John A. Mueller illustrate the stigmatization of atheist students and suggest ways for practitioners to understand and respond to this group, which may appear invisible.

In the final chapter, Sherry K. Watt discusses specific strategies for addressing defensive reactions often displayed during difficult dialogues surrounded by religious privilege.

Sherry K. Watt
Ellen E. Fairchild
Kathleen M. Goodman
Editors

References

Adler, N. "Faith and Reason on Campus." *Liberal Education*, 2007, 93(2), 20–27.
Chickering, A. W., Dalton, J. C., and Stamm, L. (eds.). *Encouraging Authenticity and Spirituality in Higher Education*. San Francisco: Jossey-Bass, 2006.
Fried, J. "Thinking Skillfully and Respecting Difference: Understanding Religious Privilege on Campus." *Journal of College and Character*, 2007, 9(1), 1–7.
Goodman, K. M., and Teraguchi, D. H. "Beyond Spirituality: A New Framework for Educators." *Diversity and Democracy*, 2008, 11(1), 10–11.

Higher Education Research Institute. *The Spiritual life of College Students: A National Study of College Students' Search for Meaning and Purpose*. 2004–2005. Retrieved Oct. 17, 2007, from http://www.spirituality.ucla.edu/Reports/index.html.

Jablonski, M. A. (ed.). *The Implications of Student Spirituality for Student Affairs Practice*. New Directions for Student Services, no. 95. San Francisco: Jossey-Bass, 2001.

Lindholm, J. A. "Spirituality in the Academy: Reintegrating Our Lives and the Lives of Our Students." *About Campus*, 2007, *12*(4), 10–17.

Love, P., Bock, M., Jannarone, A., and Richardson, P. "Identity Interaction: Exploring the Spiritual Experience of Lesbian and Gay College Students." *Journal of College Student Development*, 2005, *46*(2), 193–209.

Rogers, J. L., and Love, P. "Exploring the Role of Spirituality in the Preparation of Student Affairs Professionals: Faculty Constructions." *Journal of College Student Development*, 2007, *48*(1), 90–104.

SHERRY K. WATT is an associate professor in Graduate Programs in Student Affairs in the Division of Counseling, Rehabilitation, and Student Development, University of Iowa.

ELLEN E. FAIRCHILD is a lecturer in the Teacher Education Program in the Department of Curriculum and Instruction at Iowa State University, Ames, Iowa.

KATHLEEN M. GOODMAN is a doctoral student and research assistant at the Center for Research on Undergraduate Education at the University of Iowa.

1

This chapter defines and discusses Christian privilege, incorporates the current state of religious flux in the United States, and offers some implications for practice as student affairs practitioners work with today's college students.

Christian Privilege, History, and Trends in U.S. Religion

Ellen E. Fairchild

In her seminal essay on white privilege, McIntosh (1988) began a discussion on privilege that has taken hold in areas outside her original intent. We now talk about privilege as it pertains not only to race and gender but to religion, especially the Christian faith. The purpose of this volume is to set a foundation for understanding Christian privilege and its effects on the lives of students who either practice a different religion or spirituality or are nonbelievers. In this chapter, I present a historical perspective that elucidates the perceived role of religion in the early making of the United States as a nation. I use that history to challenge the argument that Christianity should be privileged, and the separation of religion and state blurred, because it was the wish of the nation's founders to design the United States as a Christian nation, when, in fact, it was the opposite.

The benefit of the privilege bestowed on Christians is one of normalcy for the Christian faith while marginalizing those who do not believe or practice a different faith (Blumenfeld, 2006). This normalizing effect is then used to argue that the United States is a Christian nation, and therefore Christians in some way deserve the benefits afforded them.

By applying McIntosh's framework (1988) to Christian privilege, we can similarly understand it as "a pattern of assumptions that were passed on to me as a [Christian] person" (p. 5). This set of assumptions confers benefits on Christians while denying them to those who are not of the same faith or do not believe in a higher being. The following definitions demonstrate that privilege is not necessarily earned but conferred:

NEW DIRECTIONS FOR STUDENT SERVICES, no. 125, Spring 2009 © Wiley Periodicals, Inc.
Published online in Wiley InterScience (www.interscience.wiley.com) • DOI: 10.1002/ss.302

1. A right, immunity, or benefit enjoyed only by a person beyond the advantages of most.
2. A *grant* [emphasis added] to an individual, corporation, etc. of a special right or immunity under certain conditions.
3. The principle or condition of enjoying special rights or immunities [Dictionary.com, Apr. 23, 2008].

A list of benefits for Christians in our society has been compiled by Schlosser (2003)—for example:

- It is likely that state and federal holidays coincide with my religious practices, thereby having little to no impact on my job and/or education.
- When told about the history of civilization, I can be sure that I am shown people of my religion made it what it is.
- I probably do not need to learn the religious or spiritual customs of others, and I am likely not penalized for not knowing them.
- I am probably unencumbered by having to explain why I am or am not doing things related to my religious norms on a daily basis.
- It is likely that mass media represents my religion widely AND positively.
- It is likely that I can find items to buy that represent my religious norms and holidays with relative ease (e.g., food, decorations, greeting cards, etc.).
- My religious holidays are so completely "normal" that, in many ways, they may appear to no longer have any religious significance at all.
- I can openly display my religious symbol(s) on my person or property without fear of disapproval, violence, and/or vandalism.

Schlosser clearly describes in his list the benefits extended to Christians in a society that privileges one faith over others.

The United States: A Christian Nation?

The notion that Christian privilege is to be expected because the United States is a "Christian nation" must be challenged as one that not only is incorrect, but not helpful as we look to serve students and their existential growth. Understanding the history of this privilege is necessary in order to deconstruct it. Steven Waldman's thoughtful use of primary sources in his book *Founding Faith* (2008) informs the historical perspectives in this chapter. He cogently presents his argument that it was indeed the goal of the founding fathers (among them Benjamin Franklin, George Washington, Thomas Jefferson, John Adams, and James Madison) to raise the wall of separation between church and state in order to preserve the fragile union and meet the needs of its immigrant population. By understanding this historical perspective, the normalcy of Christian privilege is disturbed, and the notion of the United States as a "Christian nation" is exposed as false. Once exposed, Christian privilege is delegitimized, forcing us to challenge it as we do gender and racial privilege.

History's Impact on Religion

It is the case that the colonizers of the United States often used religious beliefs as the rationale for settling the colonies. In particular, there are two well-known examples of this: the Puritans of Massachusetts and the Anglicans of Virginia. The impetus driving both groups of settlers was religion, specifically Protestantism. Both groups were separatists who had left England for the freedom of practicing religion precisely the way they wanted to; the Pilgrims colonized Massachusetts in hopes of fully linking church and state (Waldman, 2008).

Oppressive practices were persistent and supported by the laws established within each colony. The laws stipulated forced worship, ministers' salaries to be paid from taxpayer coffers, and voting rights that were limited to certain religious denominations. Only full members of the congregational churches could vote in civil elections. Catholics were not allowed to vote, and in fact, they were banned, as were Baptists. It was illegal to be a Quaker, punishable in some colonies by death. Other religious bodies, especially Jews, were not allowed to erect places of worship at all in Anglican Virginia.

Faith of Our Fathers

The founding fathers came to understand that there was no dominant faith, and there would likely be none. The tyranny of the colonies' Christian practices reflected the tyranny of the Crown to many people, and most people did not regularly attend church services unless they were forced to by the laws of the colony. Beginning in 1776 with Virginia and ending with Massachusetts in 1833, all of the states discontinued an official religion (Waldman, 2008).

The founding fathers, while religious in their own ways, were cognizant of the need for a national contract that would meet the needs of current citizens and foster discussions of "what works" as the country changed its religious makeup. They realized at the time of the drafting of the Declaration of Independence that immigrants were changing the religious landscape of the country (Waldman, 2008).

The Baptists and Catholics were instrumental in the fight for the separation of church and state because of the oppression they had suffered under other Christian denominations. National leaders knew that if the country was to win the Revolution and sustain the fragile Republic, there could not be religious divisiveness. They also realized that with the influx of immigrant peoples, many different religions would one day add to the national fabric. It was this desire to encourage religious vibrancy that won the day, resulting in a nation of religious people but not a country established under one denomination. The separation of religion and government is a lasting legacy of the founding fathers, who believed that such a separation not only protected the religions themselves but also sheltered individuals from the religious tyranny they had witnessed in their own lifetimes.

It is from this historical knowledge that we can debunk the fallacy of the United States as a Christian nation. By creating the false illusion that Christianity is the norm and the United States is a Christian nation, the privileging of the Christian faith leads to a divisiveness that the founding fathers were trying to avoid. Once this powerful claim topples, we can argue against Christian privilege and begin to celebrate the religious diversity that our founding fathers saw for our nation.

Current Trends

The Pew Charitable Foundation recently released a report (2008) on a survey of thousands of people residing in the United States asking them about their religious affiliation. It describes a population in flux when determining existential practice. According to the survey, more than one-quarter of American adults (28 percent) have left the faith of their childhood to practice a different religion or no religion at all. The survey finds that "the number of people who say they are unaffiliated with any particular faith today (16.1%) is more than double the number who say they were not affiliated with any particular religion as children. Among Americans ages 18–29, one-in-four say they are not currently affiliated with any particular religion" (p. 5). Immigrants are disproportionately represented within Catholicism, Islam, Hinduism, and Buddhism.

Serving Students' Needs

The results of the Pew survey provide insight into religious belief in the United States today. The combined perspectives of the historical foundation, coupled with the current situation, can help guide how to serve students in meeting their needs in the essential development of answers to the meaning of existential life questions. This section connects history and how student affairs professionals can make meaning of it for practical purposes today.

Meeting Students Where They Are. The Pew (2008) findings have particular significance as student affairs practitioners seek to facilitate the development of students. Young adults are transient with their membership in religious communities. The age statistics of the report suggest that this is happening exactly when these young people are members of our institutions of higher education. The report points out that 25 percent of the population whom student affairs professionals serve have no religion at all. We must be ready to meet students who are looking for existential meaning wherever they are in their search for their place in humanity.

As students change religious affiliations or choose to practice no religion at all, student affairs practitioners must be nimble enough to accommodate the questions that arise when such decisions are being made. Some of these questions could be "How can I tell my parents about existential choices that may be different from the ones with which I was raised" or, "Is there a way to blend new beliefs with old?" How they choose to do this will have impact on their communities as well as society at large. They must look at ways of accommodating new religions that have entered the national community through immigrants as well as facilitating young peoples' decisions about their religious practice or lack thereof. This requires a recognition of the privilege historically afforded Christians and a commitment to work against such privilege.

Know Thyself. We must use our historical knowledge to inform our future actions. Student affairs practitioners, as they look for ways to meet the existential needs of all their students, must educate themselves on the long history of religious privilege in the United States. They must factor in their own biases and beliefs and understand the privilege that comes with being a Christian, or even a religious practitioner, in the United States. Then they must study recent trends in order to understand the changeability of young people as they seek to find answers to the big questions (Parks, 2000) of life. This search is important to many students, and therefore should be important to those who work with them. History demonstrates that the United States is not a Christian nation and that separation of religion and government was designed to prevent divisiveness, not encourage it. Therefore, as we work with students, we can reconceptualize the separation of church and state by revisiting the historical journey that has led to the development of that ideal and help make progress toward one that is more inclusive of all religions and all perspectives.

Institutional Change. Getting to know students and offering the support they need may mean that institutional customs will have to change. Calendars must be reevaluated, food services must become more responsive, and campus climate must be evaluated in an effort to assist students who find meaning in ways that do not fit the Christian norm. Providing space for students to "recognize and wrestle with privilege" (Seifert, 2007, p. 15) is necessary for them to understand the perspectives of those who have been marginalized because of Christian privilege. Also, it would be useful to provide opportunities for students to research and understand U.S. history and reflect on how it undergirds institutions of higher education. The goal is not to diminish their Christian faith, but to foster a new understanding of all beliefs, as well as the existentialism of those who do not believe. In this way, student affairs practitioners will fully educate the whole student and enlarge the discussions associated with privilege that currently are taking place on campuses throughout the nation (Seifert, 2007).

A Different Definition. In a paper presented at the American Educational Research Association National Conference, Gardner (2008) alluded to the idea that the tenth multiple intelligence would pertain to the "big questions of life"—an existential intelligence. This would be a welcome addition as we look for ways to identify and serve students in their life meaning making. It normalizes religious difference as well as being more inclusive of those who do not practice a religion. Just as we use Gardner's other identified intelligences within our classrooms to discuss learning styles, we can use his tenth intelligence to begin discussions around the privilege associated with religious practice in the United States.

Because college is a time when students continue, more independently, to define themselves and their place in their larger environments, student affairs practitioners must be ready to accommodate students' shifts in perceptions about their meanings to the big questions in life. This existential quest is defined as "a chiefly 20th century philosophical movement embracing diverse doctrines but centering on analysis of individual existence in an unfathomable universe and the plight of the individual who must assume ultimate responsibility for acts of free will without any certain knowledge of what is right or wrong or good or bad" ("Existentialism," 2008).

Using existentialism instead of spiritualism accommodates both those who adhere to a belief in a higher power and those who do not. It is assumed that everyone attempts to find meaning in life. The use of inclusive language, such as existentialism, is one way to be more inclusive of all students' development.

Conclusion

The privileging of the Christian faith in the United States has worked to establish a pseudonormalcy of the one faith. This myth of normalcy associated with Christian privilege must be debunked in order to move beyond the marginalization of significant populations of students, with the goal of providing existential development for all students. To conclude, I draw on a speech given by Parker J. Palmer (1993). He asked, "Why does a passionate historian think about the dead past?" (p. 6). His conclusion is that historians look at the past to make the present richer and more meaningful to today. We have "especially rich legacies" (p. 7) in our country's history.

As we connect our history with the realities of today, we can find a place that is more comfortable for everyone. When the history of religion and the separation of church and state are known in relation to the religious realities of today, we can design a way of knowing that includes more people. We can include those of the Christian, Muslim, Hindu, and Buddhist faiths and those who do not practice a religion at all. We can meet the needs of the students who attend our institutions in much more agile ways, meeting their needs as they search for existential meaning in a world that changes from day to day.

References

Blumenfeld, W. J. "Christian Privilege and the Promotion of 'Secular' and Not-So 'Secular' Mainline Christianity in Schooling and the Larger Society." *Equity and Excellence in Education*, 2006, 39(3), 195–210.

"Existentialism." Merriam-Webster online dictionary. Retrieved Apr. 28, 2008, from http://www.merriam-webster.com.

Gardner, H. "Multiple Intelligences Theory After 25 Years: Promises, Possibilities, and Pitfalls?" Paper presented at the American Educational Research Association National Conference, New York, Mar. 24, 2008.

McIntosh, P. "White Privilege: Unpacking the Invisible Knapsack." 1988. Retrieved Apr. 23, 2008, from www.seamonkey.ed.asu.edu.

Palmer, P. J. "The Violence of Our Knowledge: Toward a Spirituality of Higher Education." Michael Keenan Memorial Lecture, Berea College, Ky., 1993.

Parks, S. D. *Big Questions, Worthy Dreams*. San Francisco: Jossey-Bass, 2000.

Pew Charitable Trust. Pew Forum on Religion and Public Life. *U.S. Religious Landscape Survey*. 2008. Retrieved Feb. 26, 2008, from http://www.pewtrusts.org/our_work_detail.aspx?id=568.

Schlosser, L. Z. "Christian Privilege: Breaking a Sacred Taboo." *Journal of Multicultural Counseling and Development*, Jan. 2003, *31*, 44–51.

Seifert, T. "Understanding Christian Privilege: Managing the Tensions of Spiritual Plurality." *About Campus*, May-June 2007, pp. 10–17.

Waldman, S. *Founding Faith: Providence, Politics, and the Birth of Religious Freedom in America*. New York: Random House, 2008.

ELLEN E. FAIRCHILD is a lecturer in the Teacher Education Program in the Department of Curriculum and Instruction at Iowa State University, Ames, Iowa.

2

This chapter discusses ways student affairs practitioners can aid students on the journey to asking and answering life's big questions. The suggestions are based on a study that compares student affairs practitioners' sense of life purpose and spiritual well-being relative to their engagement in practices associated with students' inner development.

Practical Implications for Student Affairs Professionals' Work in Facilitating Students' Inner Development

Tricia A. Seifert, Noël Holman-Harmon

In the past ten years, a growing body of research has been devoted to examining the role of spirituality in the lives of college students. Recognizing the importance of distinguishing between religion and spirituality, some have characterized spirituality in terms of students' journey or quest (see Bryant, 2006) in search of their own answers to the "big questions" (Parks, 2000)—those that deal with identity ("Who am I?"), destiny or calling ("Where am I going?"), faith ("What can I believe in?"), wholeness ("How can I be happy?"), and mattering ("Will my life make a difference?") (Dalton, Eberhardt, Bracken, and Echols, 2006). However, student affairs practitioners are still grappling with how to engage students in discussions about these questions in ways that promote students' inner development, while consciously recognizing the variability of both students' and student affairs practitioners' spiritual and religious practices and beliefs.

Despite well-meaning efforts and intentions to define spirituality in an inclusive manner, the root word, *spirit,* conveys a construct that does not resonate with all students or all student affairs practitioners. Students' inner development, which we define as their sense of living authentically with purpose and meaning, is critical and should be the concern of all student affairs practitioners. There may be a perception that practitioners

who identify as religious or spiritual are more inclined to engage in practices associated with facilitating students' inner development than those who do not. Our research tested this notion by examining the effects of student affairs practitioners' sense of life purpose and spiritual, religious, and existential well-being in their engagement in practices associated with students' inner development. We briefly review these findings before discussing practical ways student affairs practitioners can engage all students in discussions of big questions and making recommendations informed by our research.

Spirituality, Life Purpose, and Student Affairs Practice

Recent research in this area has focused on a number of issues:

- Theories of spiritual and faith development (Love, 2001, 2002; Parks, 2000; Tisdell, 2003)
- The impact and importance of religion and spirituality in students' daily lives (Astin and Astin, 2003; Bryant, 2006; Bryant, Choi, and Yasuno, 2003; Lee, 2002; Lindholm, 2006; Love, Bock, Jannarone, and Richardson, 2005; Magolda and Ebben, 2006; Moran, 2007)
- How student affairs practitioners can best support students in their development (Chickering, Dalton, and Stamm, 2006; Jablonski, 2001; Love and Talbot, 1999; Parks, 2000; Rogers and Love, 2007)
- How specific demographic groups of students can best be supported in their spiritual growth and development (Love, Bock, Jannarone, and Richardson, 2005; Watt, 2003)

Research conducted by the Higher Education Research Institute (HERI) has found that students are actively engaged and interested in issues of religion and spirituality and that they question and explore these issues during their college experience (Astin and Astin, 2003). In the light of students' interest in these issues and the long-standing tradition of the student affairs profession to address development of the whole student (Evans and Reason, 2005; Nuss, 2003), there has been increasing interest in how student affairs staff (Chickering, Dalton, and Stamm, 2006; Jablonski, 2001; Love and Talbot, 1999; Parks, 2000; Rogers and Love, 2007), as well as faculty (Lindholm and Astin, 2008; Palmer, 1993; Trautvetter, 2008), can support the spiritual and religious and inner development of college students.

We present a general description of a study we conducted and then share implications of this study for professional practice and ways this information can be used when working with students in ways that will contribute to their inner development.

A Study of Student Affairs Practitioners' Spiritual Well-Being, Life Purpose, and Professional Practice

The purpose of this study was to examine the relationship between student affairs professionals' practice and their personal sense of life purpose and spiritual well-being. We partnered with the American College Personnel Association (ACPA) to conduct this research. ACPA sent an e-mail to all graduate and professional members within the United States inviting them to participate. Participants followed a link to a secure Web site in which they completed the twenty-minute online survey. With a 26 percent response rate, the respondent sample (approximately fifteen hundred) was similar to the overall ACPA membership in terms of gender, race/ethnicity, and age. In order to measure purpose in life and spiritual well-being, we intentionally selected instruments that have been used in psychological and social science research for nearly twenty years.

The first section of the survey consisted of the fourteen-item Life Purpose scale of psychological well-being. We chose it because we felt it measured purpose in life in a secular way that did not reference God specifically or any other higher power (Ryff, 1989). The second section consisted of the Spiritual Well-Being Scale (SWBS) (Ellison, 1983; Paloutzian and Ellison, 1982), a ten-item Religious Well-Being subscale that provides a self-assessment of one's relationship with God, and the ten-item Existential Well-Being subscale, which gives a self-assessment of one's sense of life purpose and life satisfaction. Summing the two subscales provides a general indicator of spiritual well-being. The SWBS instrument uses the term *God* as a focus of that higher power, which did not resonate with all of our respondents.

The third section of the survey measured the frequency with which student affairs practitioners engage in various practices with students. Research has identified practices that promote the spiritual development of students (Cannister, 1999; Chickering, 2008; Chickering, Dalton, and Stamm, 2006; Daloz, Keen, Keen, and Parks, 1996; Dalton, Eberhardt, Bracken, and Echols, 2006; Koth, 2003; Love, 2002; Parks, 2000; Tisdell, 2003). However, we believe naming these practices as contributing to students' spiritual development may limit their application to students who identify with the term *spiritual*. For this reason, we refer to these practices as those that may contribute to students' inner development, a term we find to be more inclusive of diverse student beliefs and values.

The survey concluded with demographic questions concerning the participants and their work locations. Questions ascertained gender, race/ethnicity, age, graduate degree in student affairs, and any religious affiliation of their institution.

Practice Aligns Along Three Domains. We were interested in learning what effect spiritual well-being and life purpose had on practices in which student affairs practitioners engage students. We sought to answer this question by first seeing if relationships existed among the twenty practices. Using factor analysis, we found the items measured three general domains of practice that we then assembled into separate scales. The Community Building Scale ($\alpha = .877$) measured practitioners' use of intentional student interactions that may cause a reexamination of previous assumptions and perspective. The Modeling Authenticity Scale ($\alpha = .848$) related to practitioners' willingness to mentor students by sharing their own journey of asking and answering the big questions. The Reflective Practice Scale ($\alpha = .732$) assessed practitioners' use of creative mediums and opportunities for reflection with students. If practitioners seek to facilitate students' inner development, which many of the founding documents of the profession exhort, grounding student affairs practice in these domains is a prudent strategy.

Practitioners' Sense of Life Purpose Matters Most. After assessing what domains of practice were associated with students' inner development, we examined to what extent practitioners' sense of life purpose, spiritual well-being, existential well-being, and religious well-being affected their use of these domains in their practice. We tested a host of predictive models and found, net of other influences, that a practitioner's purpose in life had a statistically larger positive effect on the extent to which they engage in community building, modeling authenticity, and reflective practices with students than their levels of spiritual well-being, existential well-being, and religious well-being. The fact that life purpose clearly yielded the greatest influence on practitioners' willingness to engage in practices associated with students' inner development calls on practitioners to rethink the language they use to discuss inner development and reconsider their own journey in asking and answering life's big questions.

Practical Implications

In this section, we discuss what this research means in terms of addressing religious privilege and the implications for the discourse surrounding religion and spirituality for student affairs practice.

Addressing Privilege. Those who identify as spiritual (typically with a reference to God or some higher power) or religious, or both, often unfairly earn a degree of privilege due to the perception that they are more likely to engage in practices associated with students' inner development. This perception, however, is unfounded. Although those who feel spiritually called to the profession may believe a higher power gives center to their practice, it matters little whether practitioners have a spiritual grounding (with reference to God or a higher power); what matters is that they have a strong sense of meaning or purpose to their life. It is this sense of student affairs practitioners' lives that has a true impact on the way they engage with students in practices that facilitate students' inner development.

Change the Discourse. Given that life purpose matters most, we assert that higher education's recent and vociferous focus on spirituality may unwittingly perpetuate the idea that those who identify as spiritual or religious are the only ones prepared to assist students. Student affairs practitioners' disposition and understanding of their own life purpose, not their spiritual well-being, make the biggest difference in their motivation to engage in practices that build community, model authenticity, and engage students in reflective ways. If the field is sincerely resolute in using inquiry to foster holistic student learning, then it is time to change the discourse to reflect the evidence.

The term *spirituality* is particularly confusing and synonymous to many with religion (Nash, 2001), and it is often ill defined. We believe the term *inner development* is more inclusive. Some participants in our study chose not to respond to questions on the Religious Well-Being Scale because the references to God did not resonate with them. If student affairs practitioners are so put off by items referencing God or a higher power, it makes one question how their beliefs manifest in their interactions with students who have strong spiritual or religious beliefs. It also leaves one to wonder how many students embark on the "big question" journey alone because the term *spirituality* does not honor their experience and perspective. In an effort to meet all students where they are, we encourage student affairs practitioners to refocus their interactions with students around students' inner development instead of spirituality.

Student affairs practitioners may need to clearly delineate (for themselves and students) when they are discussing inner development and when they are discussing spirituality or religion. Religion may be one dimension of inner development, spirituality may be another, and the broader search to live authentically with a sense of purpose and meaning may be still another. This is not to say, however, that these dimensions are mutually exclusive. For some students (and practitioners as well), a conversation about inner development may center on a conversation about religious belief or personal spiritual practice. However, to assume that inner development has these connotations for all students removes places at the table for a host of students, particularly agnostics, atheists, freethinkers, and secular humanists, among others. If we are "to know as we are known," as Parker Palmer (1983) urges, then a welcoming and inclusive language must serve as our community's foundation.

In order to be inclusive of all students, student affairs practitioners from both ends of the spectrum (highly religious to atheist) likely need to reconceptualize and reconcile how they support students' inner development. This may require first a recognition and acknowledgment of their own stances on religious and spiritual beliefs and practices, as well as their responses to the big questions, in order to assess the effect of their biases on their work with students.

An Examined Life. In order for student affairs practitioners to be personally and professionally available to journey with students into the land of big questions, they must examine their own personal journey into student affairs work and ask themselves intentional questions about their calling as student affairs practitioners—for example:

- In what ways am I clear about what I do and the purpose behind my commitment to the student affairs profession?
- What motivates me personally toward this profession?
- What assumptions do I have about inner development or, rather, my sense of living authentically with purpose and meaning?
- What assumptions do I have about spirituality and religion?
- What role do I believe higher education should play in fostering students' inner development, particularly as this may relate to spirituality and religion for some students?
- What is my comfort zone in terms of asking (and struggling to answer) the big questions, and how does that bear on my work with all students?

Student affairs practitioners have to be willing to engage in their own inner development in order to be "good company" (Baxter Magolda, 2005) on students' inner development journeys.

A helpful start to unpacking student affairs practitioners' biases on the topics of religion, spirituality, and inner development is to create professional development opportunities focusing on these issues. Student affairs practitioners need occasions to think through their own sense of life purpose and how they are living an authentic life. They need time to think about and honestly assess their biases, how they came to those biases, and what they are willing to work on in order to best meet the needs of students. *Spirituality* is the contemporary topic of interest in higher education, and as with issues such as race and sexual orientation, student affairs professionals often shy away from conducting and honoring their self-assessments, particularly if their personal values deviate from what they perceive is the normative expectation of the profession. However, by not unpacking, confronting, and accepting our true feelings about issues such as spirituality, life purpose, and religion, we may do unintentional harm, or at the very least have a negative impact on the students with whom we work. Facilitating conversations about inner development and wrestling with big questions with students likely comes more easily to practitioners who have had the chance and taken the time to think through and wrestle with these issues themselves.

This inner development work requires a big leap for most practitioners. First, it means setting aside time that could otherwise be used on something tangible, like planning a program, to reflect and think about that which is far less tangible. It is difficult to quantify the outcomes of time spent thinking about what one's purpose is in the profession or how to act more authentically with students and coworkers. When the profession rewards only what can be seen, practitioners' inner development is devalued. However, if student affairs practitioners are truly to be "good company" on students' journeys, they must take the time to prepare their own provisions. The outcomes of this kind of inner development, while less tangible, will manifest in richer, fuller interactions with not only students but colleagues.

Practitioners' inner development work may languish if a community engaged in similar pursuits does not support and celebrate it. Convening a mentoring community (Parks, 2000) to provide a place for practitioners to grapple with the big questions and articulate, interrogate, process, and commit to a self-authored purpose is necessary. This may mean finding or creating different spaces for both practitioners and students where they feel safe to reflect on and converse about difficult issues. It may also mean establishing or creating a culture where engaging in discussions about life purpose and inner development is valued and respected as a worthy pursuit and essential to the lifeblood of the community. This may be a challenge. Our fast-paced society conditions us that time spent in reflection or in conversation is wasteful. However, recent research has shown that today's students crave the chance to explore issues of inner development (HERI, 2004–2005).

Student affairs professionals have been stewards of holistic learning, unwavering in their commitment to the development of the whole student, a concept that continues to evolve. As the needs of students change, so too must the profession. Student affairs professionals must continue to find ways, whether comfortable or not, to meet that historic edict.

Conclusion

In order to best facilitate students' inner development, students affairs practitioners need to change the discourse to reflect the diverse beliefs and values of today's college students. Attempting to repackage *spirituality* and *spiritual development* as inclusive terms denies the power and privilege that they engender for those on the margins. In order to engage in practices that reach all students, student affairs practitioners must recommit to questioning, reflecting, understanding, and, where necessary, developing their own sense of meaning and life purpose. These practitioners' own inner development affects the degree to which they engage in community building, modeling authenticity, and reflective practices—all of which have been shown to promote students' inner development. Given the resurgence of interest in facilitating students' spiritual development (which we have renamed *inner development*), it may best serve student affairs practitioners to refocus on asking and struggling with their own big questions. Only then will they have the fullest capacity to be good company for students on their inner quest and journey.

References

Astin, A. W., and Astin, H. S. "Spirituality in College Students: Preliminary Findings from a National Study." Los Angeles: Higher Education Research Institute, University of California, Los Angeles, 2003.

Baxter Magolda, M. "Helping Students Make Their Way to Adulthood: Good Company for the Journey." *About Campus,* 2002, 6(6), 2–9.

Bryant, A., Choi, J., and Yasuno, M. "Understanding the Religious and Spiritual Dimensions of Students' Lives in the First Year of College." *Journal of College Student Development,* 2003, 44(6), 723–745.

Bryant, A. N. "Exploring Religious Pluralism in Higher Education: Non-Majority Religious Perspectives Among Entering First-Year College Students." *Religion and Education,* 2006, 33(1), 1–25.

Cannister, M. W. "Mentoring and the Spiritual Well-Being of Late Adolescents." *Adolescence,* 1999, 34(136), 769–779.

Daloz, L., Keen, C. H., Keen, J. P., and Parks, S. D. *Common Fire.* Boston: Beacon Press, 1996.

Chickering, A. W. "Curricular Content, Powerful Pedagogy, and Student Activities to Encourage Spiritual Growth." Presentation at the Iowa State University's Conference on Spirituality, Ames, Mar. 2008.

Chickering, A. W., Dalton, J. C., and Stamm, L. *Encouraging Authenticity and Spirituality in Higher Education.* San Francisco: Jossey-Bass, 2006.

Dalton, J. C., Eberhardt, D., Bracken, J., and Echols, K. "Inward Journeys: Forms and Patterns of College Student Spirituality." *Journal of College and Character,* 2006, 7(8), 1–21.

Ellison, C. W. "Spiritual Well-Being: Conceptualization and Measurement." *Journal of Psychology and Theology,* 1983, 11, 330–340.

Evans, N. J., and Reason, R. D. "Guiding Principles: A Review and Analysis of Student Affairs Philosophical Statements." *Journal of College Student Development,* 2001, 42(4), 359–377.

Higher Education Research Institute (HERI). (2004–2005). "The Spiritual Life of College Students: A National Study of College Students' Search for Meaning and Purpose." Retrieved Oct. 17, 2007, from http://www.spirituality.ucla.edu/reports/index.html.

Jablonski, M. A. (ed.). *The Implications of Student Spirituality for Student Affairs Practice.* New Direction for Student Services, no. 95. San Francisco: Jossey-Bass, 2001.

Koth, K. "Deepening the Commitment to Serve: Spiritual Reflection on Service-Learning." *About Campus,* 2003, 7(6), 2–7.

Lee, J. J. "Changing Worlds, Changing Selves: The Experience of the Religious Self Among Catholic Collegians." *Journal of College Student Development,* 2002, 43(3), 341–356.

Lindholm, J. A. "The 'Interior' Lives of American College Students: Preliminary Findings from a National Study." In J. L. Heft (ed.), *Passing on the Faith: Transforming Traditions for the Next Generation of Jews, Christians, and Muslims.* New York: Fordham University Press, 2006.

Lindholm, J. A., and Astin, H. S. "Spirituality and Pedagogy: Faculty's Spirituality and Use of Student-Centered Approaches to Undergraduate Teaching." *Review of Higher Education,* 2008, 31(2), 185–207.

Love, P. G. "Spirituality and Student Development: Theoretical Connections." In M. A. Jablonski (ed.), *The Implications of Student Spirituality for Student Affairs Practice.* New Directions for Student Services, no. 95. San Francisco: Jossey-Bass, 2001.

Love, P. G. "Comparing Spiritual Development and Cognitive Development." *Journal of College Student Development,* 2002, 43(3), 357–373.

Love, P. G., Bock, M., Jannarone, A., and Richardson, P. "Identity Interaction: Exploring the Spiritual Experiences of Lesbian and Gay College Students." *Journal of College Student Development,* 2005, 46(2), 193–209.

Love, P. G., and Talbot, D. "Defining Spiritual Development: A Missing Consideration for Student Affairs." *NASPA Journal,* 1999, *37,* 361–375.

Magolda, P., and Ebben, K. "College Student Involvement and Mobilization: An Ethnographic Study of a Christian Student Organization." *Journal of College Student Development,* 2006, *47*(3), 281–298.

Moran, C. D. "The Public Identity Work of Evangelical Christian Students." *Journal of College Student Development,* 2007, *48*(4), 418–434.

Nash, R. *Religious Pluralism in the Academy: Opening the Dialogue.* New York: Peter Lang, 2001.

Nuss, E. M. "The Development of Student Affairs." In S. R. Komives and D. B. Woodward Jr. (eds.), *Student Services: A Handbook for the Profession.* (4th ed.) San Francisco: Jossey-Bass, 2003.

Palmer, P. J. *To Know as We Are Known.* San Francisco: HarperSanFrancisco, 1983.

Paloutzian, R. F., and Ellison, C. W. "Loneliness, Spiritual Well-Being and the Quality of Life." In L. A. Peplau and D. Perlman (eds.), *Loneliness: A Sourcebook of Current Theory, Research and Therapy.* Hoboken, N.J.: Wiley, 1982.

Parks, S. D. *Big Questions, Worthy Dreams.* San Francisco: Jossey-Bass, 2000.

Rogers, J. L., and Love, P. "Exploring the Role of Spirituality in the Preparation of Student Affairs Practitioners: Faculty Constructions." *Journal of College Student Development,* 2007, *48*(1), 90–104.

Ryff, C. D. "Happiness Is Everything, or Is It? Explorations on the Meaning of Psychological Well-Being." *Journal of Personality and Social Psychology,* 1989, *57,* 1069–1081.

Tisdell, E. J. *Exploring Spirituality and Culture in Adult and Higher Education.* San Francisco: Jossey-Bass, 2003.

Trautvetter, L. C. "Undergraduate Perspectives About Religion in Higher Education." In M. R. Diamond (ed.), *Encountering Faith in the Classroom: Turning Difficult Discussions into Constructive Engagement.* Sterling, VA.: Stylus Publishing, 2008.

Watt, S. K. "Come to the River: Using Spirituality to Cope, Resist, and Develop Identity." In M. F. Howard-Hamilton (ed.), *Meeting the Needs of African American Women.* New Directions for Student Services, no. 104, San Francisco: Jossey-Bass, 2003.

TRICIA A. SEIFERT is a postdoctoral research scholar in the Center for Research on Undergraduate Education at the University of Iowa.

NOËL HOLMAN-HARMON is a doctoral candidate in the student affairs administration and research program at the University of Iowa.

3

This chapter grapples with the intersections of race, culture, and religion and explores how experiences in a shared religion can be different when viewed through the lens of race and culture. Practical strategies are provided for ways student affairs practitioners can facilitate difficult dialogues around Christian privilege in concert with issues related to racial and cultural marginalization.

Difficult Dialogues at the Intersections of Race, Culture, and Religion

Dafina Lazarus Stewart, Adele Lozano

It is imperative to understand that both racial/ethnic cultural identity and religious identity may play salient roles in the lives of the individual, particularly among people of color (Brooks, 2003; McEwen, Roper, Bryant, and Langa, 1990; Silverman, 2005; Tisdell, 2003). Experiences of marginalization may be multiplied (both identities are marginalized) or divided (one identity is marginalized and the other is not) depending on the particular ways in which individuals identify racially/ethnically and religiously. To complicate matters, religious history, traditions, styles of worship, and values are often deeply integrated into people's understanding of their particular racial/ethnic cultural identity (Tisdell, 2003). As such, religious identity may not be seen as a separate identity facet at all, but rather as one aspect of how they make meaning of their racial/ethnic identities.

As individuals, we come at this topic from different places in our lives, backgrounds, and professional experiences. At this point in life, Dafina considers herself first as Christian and then as black, a person of African descent in the United States connected to African peoples around the globe by history, genealogy, and the African unconscious (Bynum, 1999). Her dogma is more closely aligned with evangelical Christianity than its more mainstream counterparts. Dafina is more drawn to the worship styles of the churches in which she grew up in Harlem, New York City, which were dominated by black, working-class, first- and second-generation migrants from the South, particularly North and South Carolina and Georgia. She grew up

NEW DIRECTIONS FOR STUDENT SERVICES, no. 125, Spring 2009 © Wiley Periodicals, Inc.
Published online in Wiley InterScience (www.interscience.wiley.com) • DOI: 10.1002/ss.304

23

very much aware of the role of the black church in community activism, the pursuit of racial justice, and the alleviation of poverty.

Adele identifies first with her ethnic background, which is Mexican American. When speaking in general terms, she identifies as Latina, which connects her with many other diverse people from Spanish-speaking countries that were historically colonized and oppressed by Europeans. However, if she is speaking with close friends or others with whom she feels a close bond she will identify as Chicana, a word that carries more political connotations. Her identity becomes more complex when language is considered because English is her first language, and as an adult, she has continued to struggle to learn conversational Spanish. She considers herself to be a spiritual person and a Christian, but does not identify strongly with a particular denomination. Although she was raised a Catholic and participated in the sacraments of baptism, first communion, and confirmation, she did not find Catholicism to be congruent with many of her values and beliefs as an adult. Her view of Catholicism evolved as she entered college and met other Chicanas/os and Latinas/os who, unlike her, grew up in more traditional Mexican homes where Spanish was the first language and Catholicism was paramount.

How we understand ourselves as people of faith is deeply informed by how we understand ourselves as people of color. Therefore, we believe that any discussion about religion and religious privilege must take into account the ways in which race, culture, nationality, and even language mediate people's religious experiences and identities. As such, religious identity may be seen not as a separate identity facet at all, but rather as one aspect of how we make meaning of our racial and ethnic identities.

In this chapter, we first highlight some of the nuances that make dialogue difficult at the intersections of race, culture, and religion. We further exemplify the complexities by using two examples from the Christian religious tradition that are viewed through the lens of African American and Mexican American culture. Finally, we provide practical suggestions for engaging in dialogue where race, culture, and religion are considered.

Race, Culture, and Religion

There is an inextricable link among race, culture, and religion in various cultural traditions. Examples can be taken from Native American, African American, and Asian cultures. When it comes to American Indian culture, the cultural-religious connection is familiar. The pow-wow, journeys, sweat lodges, and other ceremonial facets of indigenous culture in the United States are understood to represent the deep spiritual connection that native people have with the earth, the Great Spirit, and the community. The indigenous nations that occupied Turtle Island, the name for the North American continent by indigenous people (Peat, 2006), had highly developed and richly celebrated systems of religion and faith long before the arrival of the Europeans (Brooks, 2003; Silverman, 2005). The culture of First Nations people cannot be understood without also understanding the nature and system of their spirituality and religion.

Despite the acknowledged central role of the black church in the lives of African Americans, it is not usually understood that the inextricable link between culture and spirituality for Africans is similar to that of First Nations people. Black people in the United States have cultural and historical roots predominantly among the nations and peoples of western Africa. Some scholars argue that a full appreciation of the norms and traditions of black people in the United States requires an understanding of the parallels to the norms and traditions of continental Africans (Bynum, 1999; Nobles, 1980; Myers, 1993). Ideas about the nature of reality, life, and experience are held in common by many West African peoples. Particularly common is the assumption that what constitutes reality is the unity of what is spiritual (extrasensory) and what is material (sensory). Following from that is the understanding that all processes are interconnected through both human and spiritual networks, that spiritualism and communalism are appropriate values to guide behavior, and that life and space are infinite and unlimited and manifested as spirit (Bynum, 1999; Nobles, 1980; Myers, 1993). These ideas persist through African American culture and help to explain the prominence of the black church in the African American community and views of black students. Recent research suggests that some black students understand their identities as spirit manifesting through facets such as race, gender, social class, sexual orientation, and personality (Stewart, 2007).

Within Asian cultures, a wide variety of religious practices and attitudes about religion and spirituality exists. For some, particularly those within the Polynesian triangle, the interconnection of religion, spirituality, and culture is embedded. For instance, the religious identity of Korean American evangelical Christian college students may be understood in terms of their racial identity and not as discrete identity facets (Kim, 2006; Kim, 2000; Park, 2004). For these students, the representation of Christianity in their lives is interconnected with a salient Korean ethnic identity.

This literature clearly posits that religion and culture are often intertwined in the lives of individuals. However, this intersection is also reflected in the structures and practices of religious systems themselves. For this discussion, we pay particular attention to ways that the customs of Christianity reflect the nuances of the cultural contexts in which it is practiced. The difference between the cultural practices associated with Christianity and its spiritual and religious belief systems is captured in the terms *cultural Christianity* and *culturally Christian*. These terms bring to the surface the cultural aspects inherent in the practice of Christianity. The concept of cultural Christianity helps make meaning of the ways white racial privilege may shroud worship, traditions, and language that actually reflect racial and cultural inflections rather than anything that may be understood as authentically or universally "Christian" or "culturally Christian." One of the examples in the next section will explore this idea.

NEW DIRECTIONS FOR STUDENT SERVICES • DOI: 10.1002/ss

Two Examples of Christianity's Racial and Cultural Complications

Christians who are members of marginalized racial and ethnic groups may understand their religious identity within the Christian community not as a source or location of privilege but as aligned with the struggle against racial and ethnic oppression. In such cases, how are locations of privilege and oppression identified? How should student affairs professionals negotiate requests to affirm a group's racial/ethnic expression when that expression may include symbols, traditions, and language representing a religious perspective that is afforded privilege in certain social spheres in the United States to the neglect of contrasting religious perspectives in those spheres? How do we engage these difficult dialogues in ways that appreciate the multifaceted nature of privilege and oppression and incorporate cultural knowledge to design effective and appropriate interventions that encourage the mutual respect and honoring of diverse and even conflicting perspectives?

Two examples demonstrate the complications that arise when race, culture, and religion intersect and lead to implications for student affairs practice that address these questions.

Example One: Calvin College. African American faculty member Denise Isom's experience at Calvin College (Redden, 2008) reveals challenges that lie at the intersection of race, culture, and religion. Calvin College has strong ties to its founding sectarian body, the Christian Reformed church. As a result of this continued linkage, Calvin faculty are required to adhere to a three-prong test of faith: membership in a congregation of the Christian Reformed church, signing a statement of faith, and sending their children to Christian schools (Calvin College Faculty Handbook, n.d.). Isom, who had attempted to abide by this requirement, found that she no longer could and requested an exemption from the policy so that she could join a Christian congregation in a different denomination with a predominantly African American membership.

In her letter, published in part by the online periodical *Inside Higher Ed,* Isom writes, "I find myself at a place where, for emotional, social, and spiritual health, I need a place of worship that is already consistent with my culture and able to grapple with issues of race in ways which make it a respite, a recharging and growing place for me, as opposed to another location where I must 'work' and where I am 'other'" (para. 3). Discussing the situation at Calvin, Alan Wolfe (professor of political science and director of the Boisi Center for Religion and American Public Life at Boston College) was quoted as saying that "[Calvin's] faith test is essentially both religious and ethnic" due to the Dutch roots of the Christian Reformed church (Redden, para. 10). Isom's and Wolfe's remarks demonstrate the ways in which race/culture and religion are deeply interconnected and intersected, such that from a cultural standpoint, being a Christian is not solely a matter of fellowship with others who share spiritual or theological perspectives. Rather, the fellowship of Christians includes, perhaps more important for some people of color, the sharing of racial, ethnic, and cultural perspectives as well.

The situation at Calvin College points to the themes and historical context of race, culture, and religion. These elements are deeply interconnected, and notions of religious privilege have little meaning for people of color who consider themselves Christians when they have been ostracized and marginalized by whites who are also Christians. Most often, what others casually assert as Christian privilege is, in the experiences of people of color, actually white privilege and racism, which are elements that define "cultural Christianity." Martin Luther King Jr. said that Sunday morning at eleven o'clock is the most segregated hour in the United States. Research also supports this assessment, saying that less than 10 percent of Christian congregations in the United States can be classified as multiracial (Emerson and Chai Kim, 2003). The history and prevalence of racial segregation and division among American Christians make interracial and multicultural gatherings difficult, if not impossible. On campus, Christian student groups are often also characterized by the same patterns of racial segregation that exist in the larger society (Donahoo and Payne, 2008).

Implications for student affairs. Isom's experience highlights how religion, unconsciously, can result in cultural marginalization even for people who share the same faith system. Within student affairs, traditions and practices associated with religious student organizations may have the same culturally marginalizing effect. Helping students recognize that they may be attempting to impose culturally specific traditions and practices on members of their organization may disrupt the exercise of racial privilege operating under the guise of religious tradition.

Example Two: Día de los Muertos. Another example of the intersection of religion, spirituality, and culture is the Día de los Muertos (Day of the Dead) celebration, which is celebrated annually by some Latinos, particularly those of Mexican origin. Día de los Muertos blends pre-Colombian indigenous rituals with Catholic beliefs and practices into a uniquely Mexican celebration that honors deceased loved ones while recognizing death as a part of life. The concept of resistance is an important cultural/political aspect of Día de los Muertos. Although the Latina/o population consists of diverse groups, most share a history of colonialism and oppression. It is commonly believed that indigenous populations in Mexico refused to back down when the Spanish colonizers tried to force them to relinquish their annual Día de los Muertos ritual (Brandes, 1998). Many Latina/o college students are aware of this spirit of resistance and may draw parallels to their own struggles to pursue higher education in the face of institutional racism, financial hardships, and marginalization within the academy. Día de los Muertos can serve to empower students as they recognize the importance of resistance, connect with their spiritual selves, and reaffirm the value of their cultural traditions.

New Directions for Student Services • DOI: 10.1002/ss

The cultural lens through which many nonmajority cultural groups view death is a significant aspect of this celebration for student affairs professionals to consider. Día de los Muertos may appear to be a morbid or strange celebration with the building of altars, the prevalence of skulls, and an apparent focus on death combined with a festive atmosphere. In reality, it is a ritual that emphasizes the concept of duality in Mexican culture, where death is viewed as a continuation of life through the open acknowledgment of the reality of a spiritual, nonmaterial existence.

Implications for student affairs. It is important to provide a variety of opportunities for dialogue regarding how different oppressed groups have managed to retain cultural and spiritual traditions despite imperialism. Discussing a specific tradition, such as Día de los Muertos, can also help Latino/a and non-Latino/a students understand the intersection of religion and culture. However, it may be intimidating for students to approach one another to begin a meaningful dialogue around religion and culture for fear of offending someone. Student affairs practitioners should cultivate collaborative relationships with faculty members in anthropology, sociology, and history who can share their expertise with students to provide a starting point for discussion. Viewing a film is an excellent way to promote discussion regarding the impact of the clash of two cultures on religion and spirituality, especially if the film contains rich symbolism, as does *La Otra Conquista* (The Other Conquest), a film by writer/director Salvador Corrasco. This can be followed with an informal discussion facilitated by students to share their own experiences with oppression, privilege, culture, and spirituality. A safe and comfortable space, such as a cultural center, is ideal for viewing a film and engaging in difficult and sometimes deeply personal dialogue.

General Suggestions for Dialogues

The complexity of race, culture, and religion and their interconnections among privileged and marginalized identity facets in individuals' lives requires that those seeking to understand and intervene on behalf of marginalized identities be aware, knowledgeable, and skillful (Pope, Reynolds, and Mueller, 2004) when it comes to addressing perceived privilege and engaging in difficult dialogues in student affairs. Several characteristics of multicultural awareness, knowledge, and skills (Pope, Reynolds, and Mueller, 2004) play a key role in planning and implementing constructive dialogues about this topic.

Multicultural Awareness. One characteristic of multicultural awareness in the multicultural competence model bears particular relevance to this discussion of race and religion: "awareness of their own cultural heritage and how it affects their worldview, values, and assumptions" (Pope, Reynolds, and Mueller, 2004, pp. 18–19). Practitioners must first explore their own racial/cultural and religious identities and seek to understand how those facets have been intertwined in their life experiences.

For practitioners who identify as Christian, how do cultural elements inform their practice of Christianity, including liturgical styles and images and meanings made of Christian religious symbols and icons? Even practitioners who identify with other religious traditions must be careful to examine if their ideas and images of Christianity actually reflect racial or cultural practices and traditions. For example, what is considered appropriate for corporate worship (song selection and instruments played, dancing, and ecstatic utterances, for instance) varies according to cultural context, with critique of what is done in one church versus another largely being informed by one's own cultural traditions and norms. With this as a base, practitioners can then encourage students and others to take that same inward journey as they prepare to engage each other in dialogue. Openly sharing and discussing these ideas and images, allowing disagreement and clarification, can go a long way toward unmasking the intersections of privilege in operation.

Multicultural Knowledge. The following characteristic under multicultural knowledge builds on the awareness trait discussed above: "Knowledge about the ways that cultural differences affect verbal and nonverbal communication" (Pope, Reynolds, and Mueller, 2004, pp. 18–19). There is much in this chapter that will help readers gain knowledge about how cultural differences shape the experiences of Christians across lines of race and culture. However, practitioners should seek other resources that discuss the ways in which culturally informed differences in communication cross over into sacred spaces and affect liturgical styles, language, and sacred symbols among Christians of different racial/ethnic groups. Gaining such knowledge may involve visiting a variety of Christian congregations with all kinds of racial compositions in their memberships. It is not enough to think you have experienced Christianity by going to a service in only denomination, of predominantly one race. This is as critical to developing a multicultural knowledge and understanding of Christianity as it is to developing a fuller understanding of any other religious tradition.

Multicultural Skills. The "ability to differentiate among individual differences, cultural differences, and universal similarities" (Pope, Reynolds, and Mueller, 2004, Table 1.1) is an essential skill for a practitioner facilitating dialogue around issues of race and religious privilege. Certainly Christians universally share some things in common. However, there is a great deal more that reflects cultural differences and individual preferences. Having a truly multicultural perspective of Christianity will enable a practitioner to practice this skill effectively. It may be necessary for a practitioner to help students seemingly stuck in conflict to recognize that their differences of opinion may be informed by their cultural values or individual preferences, and disagreement is not an indictment of faith or belief. In addition, this skill is useful in working with students who may be disparaging another group's Christian religious expression as inauthentic.

Conclusion

Cultural and religious traditions may overlap and intersect in the identities and meaning-making processes of students of color. Religious and spiritual traditions may provide language for resistance and affirmation for students of color. Therefore, such students may experience their religion and spirituality differently from white students, even if they seem to share overarching identifiers, such as "Christian." This "cultural Christianity" requires practitioners and researchers to walk a fine line in understanding, interpreting, and applying concepts of privilege, power, and inclusion. Having difficult dialogues that bridge race and religion requires practitioners to develop multicultural competence, including recognizing within-group differences and understanding how multiple identities can color interactions among people who claim the same religious identity (Pope, Reynolds, and Mueller, 2004).

References

Abes, E. S., Jones, S. R., and McEwen, M. K. "Reconceptualizing the Model of Multiple Dimensions of Identity: The Role of Meaning-Making Capacity in the Construction of Multiple Identities." *Journal of College Student Development,* 2007, *48*(1), 1–22.

Brandes, S. "The Day of the Dead, Halloween, and the Quest for Mexican National Identity." *Journal of American Folklore,* 1998, *111*(442), 359–380.

Brooks, J. *American Lazarus: Religion and the Rise of African-American and Native American Literatures.* New York: Oxford University Press, 2003.

Bynum, E. B. *The African Unconscious: Roots of Ancient Mysticism and Modern Psychology.* New York: Teachers College Press, 1999.

Calvin College. (n.d.). *Faculty Handbook.* Retrieved May, 28, 2008, from http://www.calvin.edu/admin/provost/fac_hb/chap_3/3_6.htm.

Donahoo, S., and Payne, S. L. "Spirituality, Religiosity, and Campus Life for Multiple Identities." Paper presented at the ACPA Conference on Multiracial and Multiple Identities, St. Louis, Feb. 8, 2008.

Emerson, M. O., and Chai Kim, K. "Multiracial Congregations: An Analysis of Their Development and a Typology. *Journal for the Scientific Study of Religion,* 2003, *42*(2), 217–227.

Kim, R. *God's Whiz Kids: Korean American Evangelicals on Campus.* New York: New York University Press, 2006.

Kim, S. "Creating Campus Communities: Second-Generation Korean-American Ministries at UCLA." In R. W. Flory and D. E. Miller (eds.), *GenX Religion.* New York: Routledge, 2000.

McEwen, M. K., Roper, L. D., Bryant, D. R., and Langa, M. J. "Incorporating the Development of African-American College Students into Psychosocial Theories of Student Development." *Journal of College Student Development,* 1990, *31*(5), 429–436.

Myers, L. J. *Understanding an Afrocentric Worldview: An Introduction to Optimal Psychology.* Dubuque, Iowa: Kendall/Hunt, 1993.

Nobles, W. W. "African Philosophy: Foundations for Black Psychology." In R. L. Jones (ed.), *Black Psychology.* New York: HarperCollins, 1980.

Park, S. "'Korean American Evangelical': A Resolution of Sociological Ambivalence Among Korean American College Students." In T. Carnes and F. Yang (eds.), *Asian American Religions: The Making and Remaking of Borders and Boundaries.* New York: New York University Press, 2004.

Peat, F. D. *Blackfoot Physics: A Journey into the Native American Universe.* Newburyport, Mass.: Weiser Books, 2006.

Pope, R. L., Reynolds, A. L., and Mueller, J. A. *Multicultural Competence in Student Affairs*. San Francisco: Jossey-Bass, 2004.

Redden, E. "When Identity Trumps Diversity." *Inside Higher Ed,* Jan. 4, 2008. Retrieved May, 28, 2008, from http://www.insidehighered.com/news/2008/01/04/calvin.

Silverman, D. J. *Faith and Boundaries: Colonists, Christianity, and Community Among the Wampanoag Indians of Martha's Vineyard, 1600–1871*. Cambridge: Cambridge University Press, 2005.

Stewart, D. L. "Perceptions of Multiple Identities Among Black College Students." Unpublished manuscript, 2007.

Stewart, D. L. "Being All of Me: Black Students Negotiating Multiple Identities." *Journal of Higher Education,* 2008, 79(2), 183–207.

Tisdell, E. J. *Exploring Spirituality and Culture in Adult and Higher Education*. San Francisco: Jossey-Bass, 2003.

DAFINA LAZARUS STEWART *is an assistant professor in the Higher Education and Student Affairs Department at Bowling Green State University.*

ADELE LOZANO *is assistant dean and director of the Latino Cultural Center at the University of Illinois, Urbana-Champaign.*

NEW DIRECTIONS FOR STUDENT SERVICES • DOI: 10.1002/ss

4

This chapter discusses issues surrounding Americans who identify with Judaism and Jewish student identity development, presents challenges Jewish students face on American college campuses, and offers strategies for faculty and administrators to use when working with Jewish undergraduates.

Working with Jewish Undergraduates

Warren J. Blumenfeld, Jacqueline R. Klein

The Jewish student population has received little attention on campuses and has indicated their disappointment with college administrators and faculty who do not understand their identity (MacDonald-Dennis, 2006a). Jewish undergraduates face many identity issues related to being Jewish (MacDonald-Dennis, 2006; Pearl, 2005), yet they have limited opportunities to learn about the impact of religion on their identity. There are limited opportunities on most campuses for Jewish students to learn about the historical and current issues related to their identities (Blumenfeld, 2006a; MacDonald-Dennis, 2006a). We present information on Jewish student identity and the historical context of Jews in the United States. For college educators to effectively work with Jewish students, it is crucial that they demonstrate an understanding of both topics.

Jewish Student Identity

Jewish identity is multifaceted and complex. For example, although Jews are members of every so-called race, dominant groups have constructed Jews across a wide spectrum on the racial divide. Many U.S. Jews often find themselves questioning the racial space they occupy, given that most European-heritage Jews (Ashkenazim) are afforded white-skinned privilege but understand that Jews have been historically seen as racialized others (Blumenfeld, 2006b; MacDonald-Dennis, 2006a). The reality is that "race," as it is currently constructed in the United States, represents a binary frame from which people of color and white people appear on opposing poles. "Race" for Jews is actually constructed on a continuum or spectrum. Once constructed as the

"other" in European society, Jews and "Jewishness"—while certainly not fully embraced by the ruling elite as "one of their own"—became a sort of middle status, "standing somewhere between the dominant position of the white majority and the marginal position of people of color" (Biale, Galchinsky, and Heschel, 1998, p. 5).

This change in Jewish ethnoracial assignment has occurred only within the past sixty or so years. According to Brodkin (1998), the changes in Jewish ethnoracial assignments over the past one hundred years have affected the ways in which Jews of different generations growing up in different eras construct their ethnoracial identities: "Those changes give us a kind of double vision that comes from racial middleness: of an experience of marginality vis-à-vis whiteness, and an experience of whiteness and belonging vis-à-vis blackness" (pp. 1–2). Kaye/Kantrowitz (1992) asserted that the ethnoracial identity of Jews complicates things. *Jewish* is both a distinct and overlapping category with polarizations of both white and color that set Jews outside the current binary frame. Therefore, Jews confound established notions of identity because of the complexity of Jewish identity. College students today often find it difficult to reconcile the relationships among their ethnic, religious, "racial," and class backgrounds and how these connect to their overall Jewish identities within the United States (Blumenfeld, 2006a; MacDonald-Dennis, 2007).

It is important to examine issues around anti-Semitism with Jewish students in higher education as well as to help students learn about oppressions of and stereotypes about Jews. Jewish students are often vitally interested in understanding the nature and impact that anti-Semitism may have on their lives (MacDonald-Dennis, 2007).

History of Oppression

After millennia of Jewish history, Jews as a community often carry contradictory notions of Jewish identity: one of an "oppression mentality," an "enemy memory" (S. Steele quoted in Berman, 1994), or a "siege mentality" (Hertzberg, in Feagin and Feagin, 1993, p. 167). This is their intense awareness that anti-Jewish oppression can surface at any time, regardless of how "good" conditions for Jews appear at any given historical moment:

> What is the first lesson a Jew learns? That people want to kill Jews. . . . To be a Jew in America, or anywhere, today is to carry with you the consciousness of limitless savagery. It is to carry that consciousness with you not as an abstraction, but as a reality; not, G*d help us all, only as memory, but also as possibility [Fein, 1988, pp. 59–60].

Many Jews are therefore forever vigilant, forever concerned, and forever anxious about the future, even in times of relative security and prosperity.

The paradox is that though many Jews learn about their history of persecution, they often are given the contradictory, though simultaneously arising, message of not talking about it, especially since the horrors of the German Holocaust. Along with this collective sense of persecution, many Jews, and in particular Jewish youth, simultaneously carry with them a history of Jewish liberatory praxis, success, and privilege as Jews, growing up in an era where wide-scale persecution against Jews in the United States has become less visible, while still surfacing on occasion in somewhat more subtle forms.

Those who do not or cannot conform to mainstream standards and are often the victims of systematic oppression are susceptible to the effects of internalized oppression, whereby they internalize, consciously or unconsciously, attitudes of inferiority or subjugation. In the case of religious minorities, this can result in low self-esteem, shame, depression, prejudiced attitudes toward members of their own religious community, and pressure to convert to the dominant religion (Bartky, 1979). Conversions to other religious denominations are but one form of assimilation; another is intermarriage. In 1957, for example, 3.5 percent of all Jews married non-Jews. By the 1980s, Jews married non-Jews as often as they married Jews (Bartky, 1979).

Implications for Working with Jewish Students

For campus educators to work effectively with Jewish students on college campuses requires an understanding of the issues contributing to Jewish identity development and the elements of the historical context. Jewish college students have reported that they are discouraged that college administrators and faculty do not understand their identity and the issues they face (Blumenfeld, 2006a; MacDonald-Dennis, 2006). According to the National Jewish Population Survey (2001), increasing numbers of younger Jewish Americans are engaging in certain religious practices, such as lighting Shabbat candles and keeping kosher, and are using the Internet to seek information on Jewish issues.

Jewish students come to college with a diversity of interests and skills (Sax, 2002). In the United States, Jewish first-year students largely attend campuses farther away from home and in residential settings at higher rates than non-Jewish students (Sax, 2002). However, it is unclear whether the group attends institutions with a larger Jewish population than in their hometown or a smaller Jewish-populated area. When deciding which college to attend, first-year students who identify with Judaism often explore Hillels (Jewish campus organizations) as an opportunity to focus on their Jewish identity (Sax, 2002). Students who participate in Jewish student campus organizations such as Hillel feel more of a sense of belonging and comfort on their campuses (Jacobson, 2001).

Another characteristic of some Jewish students is that they often tend to come from a highly educated and economically privileged background (Feagin and Feagin, 1993; Sax, 2002), which may help to explain the higher academic achievement among members of this group (Feagin and Feagin, 1993). Parents of some Jewish students are often able to invest more resources into education for their children. While this may be the case for a number of Jewish students, it should not be assumed to be the case for all. Many Jewish students come from less affluent backgrounds where resources are very limited and they are continually stressed by economic concerns.

Facilitating Difficult Dialogues About Jewish Identity

When facilitating dialogues about Jewish identity, student affairs professionals need to consider the complex notions related to the ethnic/racial, national, and religious identity of Jewish students (MacDonald-Dennis, 2007).

Using the frame of intergroup dialogues is one approach to facilitating difficult dialogues. The major goals of these dialogues are to engage students in an educational process that encourages conversation, inquiry, conflict exploration and resolution, finding common ground, and building alliances in the context of social systems of privilege and oppression. Participants learn more about their own and other cultures, histories, and experiences; learn to question prior misinformation, stereotypes, and biases; and identify actions that contribute to the creation of socially just communities (Zuniga, Nagda, and Sevig, 2002). Some campuses have developed dialogues specifically on issues around religion and religious privilege (Fairchild and Blumenfeld, 2007).

Practical Strategies for Working with Jewish Students

While it is not the intention here to give a comprehensive narrative on how to work with all Jewish undergraduates, some foundational guidelines for student affairs professionals are considered:

- *Assessment.* Hold public hearings, conduct interviews, or distribute research surveys in your institution to assess the needs, concerns, and life experiences of members of the Jewish campus community.
- *Campus climate.* Help Jewish college students feel welcome on campus by offering a supportive environment where connections can be made with other Jews through student organizations like Hillel and Jewish sororities and fraternities, as well as organizations and individuals within surrounding off-campus communities. Encourage Jewish students to explore their religious identities by participating in educational trips to Israel such as Birthright, which offers trips to Israel for Jews throughout the world.
- *Religious observances.* Campuses should offer opportunities to observe Jewish holidays through prayer services and religious foods, and kosher foods should be available.
- *Library collections.* Develop and maintain up-to-date and appropriate collections of books, videos and DVDs, and other academic materials pertaining to world religions, including Judaism, and nonbelievers.
- *Educational forums.* Organize and sponsor communitywide forums, speakers, workshops, and conferences to discuss issues related to Jewish stu-

NEW DIRECTIONS FOR STUDENT SERVICES • DOI: 10.1002/ss

dents. Also, at campus diversity fairs, Jewish students may display information about their beliefs and traditions could become annual events.

- *Continuing self-education:*

Educate yourself on issues related to Judaism in the United States and other countries throughout the world.

Without having the expectation that it is their responsibility to teach you, listen to and truly hear the voices of Jewish individuals when they relate their experiences to you.

Put yourself in the shoes of Jewish individuals, especially during major Christian holiday seasons. Attempt to experience those seasons from their perspectives. What do you perceive? Ask yourself the next time you automatically wish a Jewish person a Merry Christmas or Happy Easter, or when you are about to send a Jew a Christmas or even a season's greeting card, whether the person would truly welcome the gesture, or whether you might be imposing your traditions and values on that person.

Attend Jewish cultural and religious events.

Work for and vote for political candidates who take positions in support of religious pluralism.

Conclusion

Jewish students on college and university campuses throughout the United States comprise a vibrant, diverse, and largely invisible minority. Some Jews on many levels and for many historical, social, cultural, and economic reasons maintain a bicultural identity.

Many Jews have the opportunity to make choices about when, how, where, or whether to reveal their Jewish identities. Thus, if they choose not to reveal themselves, it is likely that others may mistake them for someone other than Jewish.

A number of strategies have been offered to assist Jewish students in positively constructing their identities and for improving the campus climate. A central tenet of Jewish tradition sums up this potential. Known as *Tikkun Olam*, it represents the process of transforming, healing, and repairing the world so that it becomes a more just, peaceful, nurturing, and perfect place. Everyone can join together to make campuses a more nurturing, perfect, and welcoming place for people of all social identities and backgrounds. We can all join and go out into our lives and onto our campuses and work for *Tikkun Olam*. We can transform the world.

References

Bartky, S. L. "On Psychological Oppression." In S. Bishop and M. Weinzweig (eds.), *Philosophy and Women.* Belmont, Calif.: Wadsworth, 1979.

Berman, P. "Introduction: The Other and the Almost the Same." In P. Berman (ed.), *Blacks and Jews: Alliances and Arguments.* New York: Dell, 1994.

NEW DIRECTIONS FOR STUDENT SERVICES • DOI: 10.1002/ss

Biale, D., Galchinsky, M., and Heschel, S. *Insider/Outsider: American Jews and Multiculturalism.* Berkeley: University of California Press, 1998.

Blumenfeld, W. J. "Christian Privilege and the Promotion of 'Secular' and Not-So 'Secular' Mainline Christianity in Public Schooling and in the Larger Society." *Equity and Excellence in Education,* 2006a, *39*(3), 195–210.

Blumenfeld, W. J. "Outside/Inside/Between Sides: An Investigation of Ashkenazi Jewish Perceptions of Their 'Race.'" *Multicultural Perspectives: Journal of the National Association for Multicultural Education,* 2006b, *8*(3), 11–18.

Brodkin, K. *How Jews Became White Folks and What That Says About Race in America.* New Brunswick, N.J.: Rutgers University Press, 1998.

Dalton, J. C. "Career and Calling: Finding a Place for the Spirit in Work and Community." *The Implications of Student Spirituality for Student Affairs Practice.* New Directions for Student Services, Fall 2001, *95,* 17–25.

Fairchild, E. E., and Blumenfeld, W. J. "Traversing Boundaries: Dialogues on Christian Privilege, Religious Oppression, and Religious Pluralism Among Believers and Non-Believers." *College Student Affairs Journal,* 2007, *26*(2), 177–185.

Feagin, J., and Feagin, C. *Racial and Ethnic Relations.* Upper Saddle River, N.J.: Prentice Hall, 1993.

Fein, L. *Where Are We? The Inner Life of American Jews.* New York: HarperCollins, 1988.

Jacobson, J. "The New Hillel: It's Not Just About Praying Anymore." *Chronicle of Higher Education,* Apr. 27, 2001, p. 33a.

Kaye/Kantrowitz, M. *The Issue Is Power: Essays on Women, Jews, Violence, and Resistance.* San Francisco: Aunt Lute Books, 1992.

Laurence, P. "Can Religion and Spirituality Find a Place in Higher Education?" *About Campus, 1999, 4*(5), 11–16.

MacDonald-Dennis, C. "Understanding Anti-Semitism and Its Impact: A New Framework for Conceptualizing Jewish Student Identity." *Equity and Excellence in Education,* 2006, *39,* 267–278.

MacDonald-Dennis, C. "Complicating Diversity Categories: Jewish Identity in the Classroom." *Diversity Digest,* 2007, *10*(2). Retrieved Jan. 10, 2008, from http://www. diversityweb.org/digest/vol10no2/macdonald-dennis.cfm.

National Jewish Population Survey. *New York: United Jewish Communities.* 2001. Retrieved Jan. 10, 2008, from http://www.ujc.org/page.html?ArticleID=33650.

Pearl, J. "Formula Could Combat Campus Racism." *Jewish Journal,* 2005. Retrieved Jan. 10, 2008, from http://www.jewishjournal.com/.

Sax, L. J. *America's Jewish Freshmen: Current Characteristics and Recent Trends Among Students Entering College.* Los Angeles: Higher Education Research Institute, University of California, Los Angeles, 2002.

Zuniga, X., Nagda, B. A., and Sevig, T. "Intergroup Dialogue: An Educational Model for Cultivating Engagement Across Differences." *Equity and Excellence in Education,* 2002, *35*(1), 7–17.

WARREN J. BLUMENFELD is an assistant professor in the Department of Multicultural and International Studies at Iowa State University.

JACQUELINE R. KLEIN is the undergraduate program administrator in the Mathematics Department at the New York University Courant Institute of Mathematical Sciences.

5

This chapter offers practical steps for creating and navigating difficult dialogues with respect to sexuality and religion. It suggests that partnership with departments, programs, and scholars of religious studies may prove helpful for student affairs professionals.

Facilitating Dialogue on Religion and Sexuality Using a Descriptive Approach

Richard W. McCarty

Student discussions on religion and sexuality are difficult dialogues to navigate due to the deeply personal nature of religious and sexual identity. This difficulty suggests a need for a helpful approach to discussions on these topics that encourages participation from a wide variety of religious and moral perspectives that students bring to the table.

As a specialist in sexual ethics from religious perspectives, I encourage student affairs professionals to engage in discussions on religion and sexuality using a descriptive approach. This approach seeks to describe a viewpoint rather than making a prescription concerning what ought to be. Using the descriptive approach on matters of religion and sexuality maximizes mutual understanding between students who come from different religious, philosophical, and moral backgrounds. A descriptive approach also allows student groups of people with a wide variety of sexual identities to engage the topic of sexuality in a way that does not alienate or privilege one sexual orientation over another. It is possible to talk descriptively about what religious traditions have to say about sex and sexuality in such a way that a wide variety of perspectives on human sexuality can be fairly explored without endorsing what a particular religious tradition might teach to its adherents.

Partnerships with religious studies departments, programs, or individual scholars can provide student affairs professionals with relevant resources

NEW DIRECTIONS FOR STUDENT SERVICES, no. 125, Spring 2009   © Wiley Periodicals, Inc.
Published online in Wiley InterScience (www.interscience.wiley.com) • DOI: 10.1002/ss.306

for designing discussions on religion and sexual orientation that are descriptive in nature.

The Need for a Descriptive Approach

Interest in investigating the intersection of religion and sexuality with students can stem from student initiatives to talk about sexuality, religion, and ethics, as well as how these facets of life contribute to personal identity. Creating such a dialogue for students is admittedly a difficult endeavor. Many liberal arts institutions have diversity policies that welcome and protect lesbian, gay, bisexual, and transgender (LGBT) students. Even so, there are students on campuses who come from religious traditions that do not agree with inclusive institutional policies.

To have a meaningful dialogue about religion and sexuality raises the risk of alienating any number of students because of their moral or religious grounding. For example, a conservative evangelical who is told that she must accept her LGBT classmates may interpret that as an effort to dismiss her faith or force her to abdicate a plank of her religious morality in favor of a policy that she cannot in faith support. And to tell LGBT students (or heterosexual allies) that they must accept the moral pontifications of a religious view that condemns their sexual identity (and morality) would likely be taken as an act of moral censure, not to mention an act of discrimination. To complicate matters, some student program developers feel ill prepared to moderate a discussion that would adequately treat the intersection of religion and sexuality. Mindful of all the ways such a discussion could go wrong, it is understandable that many faculty and student affairs professionals might feel paralyzed to address religion and sexuality at all.

Feeling paralyzed to speak adequately with respect to religion and sexuality is understandable, but it is not the uncomfortable reality that must endure. Safe space can indeed be created in order to have meaningful dialogue on religion and sexuality. To do so, however, it is necessary to draw on descriptive analyses of religion and sexuality. Although descriptive analyses seek to describe a subject or viewpoint accurately, prescriptive analyses concern what ought to be. Religious traditions often teach prescriptively, enshrining what each tradition takes to be good, holy, or of the highest value, including teachings concerning human sexuality.

Understanding, not endorsement, is the motivation behind a descriptive approach. When it is clear that dialogue on religion and sexuality is being offered using a descriptive framework, students can be invited into dialogue that allows many voices to be heard on this topic without fear of moral or theological judgment. Indeed, when students are brought into a dialogue that grounds itself in a descriptive approach, they will not only hear many voices on the subject matter but will likely come to understand (at least intellectually) why religious traditions teach what they do on human sexuality. Descriptive dialogue on religion and sexuality thus allows a wide variety of students to work together toward the common goal of understanding a diversity of ideas, rather than defending personal ideals.

Discussing Sexuality and Religion

Grounding constructive dialogue on religion and sexuality within a descriptive approach requires a starting place of some kind. One helpful place to begin is to recognize points of conflict that keep people from understanding one another when talking about religion and sexuality. Consider, at least, two such points of conflict: terminological differences and religious privilege.

Terminological Differences. In a dialogue on sexuality, in particular homosexual orientation, it is important to recognize that not everyone is working from the same lexicon. Terms such as *homosexuality, homosexual,* and *gay* mean different things to different people. Being mindful (and clear) about how terms are being defined is itself a useful tool by which it is possible to understand why people are using the terms that they do. Indeed, we can help students understand the importance of terminology in dialogues on religion and sexuality by giving them examples according to which they can reflect on their own use of the terms. Student affairs professionals might consider reflecting with students on how religious authorities define homosexuality. Indeed, the student affairs professional may find it helpful to have a discussion with students about the terminological genesis of *homosexuality* and how different religious traditions have used the term since it was coined. I offer some descriptions of terminological use as an example that student affairs professionals can draw on.

Karl Maria Kertbeny, a nineteenth-century German social scientist, coined the term *homosexual* as a categorization of human sexuality (Feray and Herzer, 1990). Based on observation, Kertbeny made the argument that some human beings have an innate, natural sexual disposition that motivates them to be sexually attracted to members of the same physical sex. Kertbeny thus considered homosexuality to be (more or less) normal, not deviant.

Alternatively, the Sacred Congregation for the Doctrine of Faith (an official teaching arm of the Catholic church) uses the term *homosexual* (or *homosexuality*) to describe tendencies that come "from a false education, from a lack of normal sexual development, from habit, from bad example, or from other similar causes, and is transitory or at least not incurable" (Sacred Congregation for the Doctrine of Faith, 1975). The Sacred Congregation also admits a second possible definition of *homosexuality,* claiming that homosexuality in some people might be a tragic pathological disorder and therefore incurable. Given such strikingly dissimilar uses of the term *homosexual* from the historical record, there are some practical lessons that can be learned (and applied) so as to help with contemporary discussions on religion and sexuality.

Practical suggestions for terminological differences. Do not assume that students come with uniform definitions of homosexuality. It is likely that students will be coming to dialogues on religion and sexuality with very different understandings of what it means to be homosexual. It will be help-ful for student affairs professionals to talk with students about how they have been using the relevant terms and where they learned the definitions that they are using. Encourage students to engage in storytelling about when they first heard the term *homosexual, homosexuality,* or other associated terms. Ask them to share the connotations of those terms. Ask the students if their understand-ing of homosexuality has changed throughout their education. If yes, explore how and why.

The point is not to get caught up in a debate to prescribe a definition of homosexuality for students, but rather to demonstrate that different tra-ditions or organizations define homosexuality differently. Descriptively, it can be said that *homosexuality,* as a term, has a traceable and specific defin-ition. In its original use, and today as well, it is very much a clinical (or spe-cialists') term. According to professional mental and physical health organizations, homosexuality is not a choice; moreover, it is not an appro-priate descriptive term for sexual behavior between people of the same sex (American Psychological Association, n.d.). Rather, homosexuality consists of innate dispositions toward a person of the same physical sex that is not only sexual, but also involves the emotional care of that person, a disposi-tion that concerns human relationships, not solely sexual acts (American Psychological Association, n.d.).

It can also be descriptively said that some institutions choose to use the term *homosexual* (or *homosexuality*) in a decidedly different way from what Kertbeny suggested, as well as what the specialists currently maintain. When considering alternative definitions, such as the one provided by the Sacred Congregation for the Doctrine of Faith, one finds that *homosexuality* is sometimes used to describe people who choose to have sex with people of the same sex. This use tends to leave out attention to human feelings, meaning, and value that precede sexual activity, and often we find the use of the term *homosexual* (or *homosexuality*) in this way to denote a kind of perversion, rebellion, or sinfulness. To reiterate, the point is only to demon-strate that it is necessary for students to understand how these terms are being used. Without such clarity, a discussion on homosexuality will likely remain confusing. However, descriptively raising awareness of how differ-ent groups use these terms may yield a measure of better understanding—even if the students fundamentally disagree with one another on the use of the terms, as well as their moral and social implications.

Religious Privilege. Dialogue on religion and sexuality also requires vigilance to religious privilege. Student affairs professionals, as well as faculty members, are likely familiar with and well trained in the social prob-lems associated with privilege. Whether stemming from a majority-dominated social ordering or from that of an elite aristocracy, privileged positions, whether social, economic, racial, and/or gender, function (pur-posefully or ignorantly) to keep out other points of view or the inclusion of minority subsets. Within a religious tradition, those theological, doctrinal, ritual, social, and moral positions that are privileged are held up under the banner of orthodoxy (right belief) or orthopraxy (right practice). Within a religious tradition, communities of faith are free to make these kinds of privileges or distinctions. Indeed, definitions of orthodoxy and orthopraxy help differentiate religious traditions one from the other. Within difficult dialogues about religion and sexuality, it is not necessary to critique why or how a religious tradition privileges doctrine or practice within its own community. Such is a freedom of religious expression rightly defended.

Concern should, however, be given to religious privilege insofar as majority, or dominant, religious traditions are uncritically assumed by students, student affairs professionals, or faculty to be the standard or best representation of religious thinking, teaching, or practice, as it relates to this issue (or any other). If a descriptive approach is to ground student dialogue on religion and sexuality, then it is necessary that the dialogue resist assumptions about sexuality that might be inherited uncritically from dominant religious traditions.

Practical suggestions for religious privilege. Resist religious privileging of any kind. The dominant religious tradition does not matter so much as awareness of it does. In a community where a progressive or liberal expression of religion was dominant, it would be necessary to carefully represent religious points of view that taught otherwise. Descriptive analyses of religious traditions do not seek to help along any one religious tradition. Rather, descriptive analyses of religious views on homosexuality would seek to see the whole of the religious landscape, rather than privileging one part of it, even if practical restraints of time and resources demand that programs cover only a certain few religious traditions and their teachings on human sexuality.

Know the demographic, and be prepared to offer relevant contrasting views. Imagine a forum has been planned on religion and sexuality for students to learn and discuss religious teachings on sexuality. Hypothetically, suppose that a number of the attendees happen to match the dominant Catholic demographic of the wider community. In the discussion, it will likely be the case that a number of attendees will rehearse the procreative norm of the Catholic tradition. If the leaders of the forum are aware of how the conversation has begun to privilege a Catholic perspective, it would then be possible to encourage a wider view of the religious landscape on human sexuality by introducing other religious teachings that may have some relevance to the discussion. For example, in this hypothetical situation, the attendees may find it interesting to learn about a well-respected rabbinical teaching in the Jewish tradition that married couples need not be open to procreation in every instance of sexual activity (Biale, 1999). The attendees may also be interested to learn that the Jewish tradition has religious teachings that oblige men to be mindful of pleasing their wives sexually, quite apart from a procreative concern (Biale, 1999). What is more, the attendees may also be intrigued to learn that in Reform Judaism (as well as in some Conservative synagogues), lesbian, gay, bisexual, and transgender relationships are affirmed and blessed as holy (Robinson, 2000). Likewise, it might be mentioned that mainline Protestant and progressive evangelical traditions (both within the wider Christian tradition) do not teach a procreative norm and in fact sanction a variety of sexual, romantic, and familial relationships (Farley, 1994; Nelson, 1978). Thus, when student dialogue on religion and sexuality is grounded in a descriptive approach, it is possible to avoid religious privilege and treat religious traditions with equal descriptive effort and respect.

Collaborating with Religious Studies Programs

In order to make dialogues on religion and sexuality possible for students, in particular, dialogues grounded in a descriptive approach, it is not necessary for student affairs professional to reinvent the wheel as it relates to the study of or scholarship on religion and sexuality. Religious studies is an interdisciplinary academic field that considers the religious dimensions of human life on a number of levels. It is usually the case that religious studies departments or programs understand that their mandate is not to indoctrinate students in theological matters, but to help students understand the history and teaching of a variety of religious traditions. A growing number of religious studies specialists concentrate their scholarship on religion and sexuality.

Student affairs professionals who partner with local religious studies departments, programs, or individual scholars will find an important resource for creating and facilitating dialogue on religion and sexuality with and for students. Many colleges and universities have religious studies departments, programs, and scholars, and some of these will likely have the resources to engage in a descriptive approach of religious teaching on sex and sexuality (and can do so from a variety of religious traditions). Partnership with a religious studies department, program, or specialist can take a variety of forms:

- *Invite a religious studies faculty member to offer a special lecture for a student program.* Student affairs specialists can take the pressure off themselves from having to learn the history and teachings of religious traditions on sexual morality by asking a religious studies specialist to offer that talk. These scholars can offer an in-depth descriptive approach to religious teaching on sexuality and be available for a question-and-answer session with the students.
- *Invite a panel of respected local clergy with a religious studies scholar to offer a closing response.* Clergypersons can often give nuanced and lively insights into religious teaching. It may prove interesting to students to hear from a wide range of religious leaders on how their religious traditions treat the subject of human sexuality, in particular homosexuality. Such a panel presentation would be augmented (and perhaps stabilized) by a response from a religious studies scholar who could summarize and analyze the discussion for the students—and offer those points of analy-

sis as material for further thought or discussion. Where clergypersons would be invited to describe the teachings of their religious traditions, the religious studies scholar could offer commentary on teachings that might help students see how the various clergypersons have represented particular views and how those views fit within the larger (and diverse) religious landscape. The religious studies scholar could also help to identify relevant points of view that were not represented by the clergypersons themselves.

• *Work with a religious studies scholar on program development.* Finding a religious studies scholar willing to plan a program with a student affairs professional would create a partnership that not only would result in a particular student event, but would also encourage the kind of faculty-staff partnership that many student affairs professionals see as the ideal coordinated effort that most benefits students' personal, moral, and academic development (American College Personnel Association [ACPA], 1996). Thus, with respect to dialogue on religion and sexuality, a coordinated effort between a student affairs professional and a religious studies scholar would help train the religious studies scholar in matters of student development and would provide a student affairs specialist an opportunity to train in the discipline of religious studies. If such a scholar is not available locally, access to such a scholar or specialist is accessible through various professional associations (for example, the American Academy of Religion).

Conclusion

Dialogue on religion and sexuality is difficult because these topics consist of deeply seated concepts of self, as well as one's relationship to other selves in the world. Perhaps this is especially true for students as they engage in self-exploration, whether by challenging boundaries, clinging to traditions, or exploring new avenues of being. When students sense that someone is challenging their sense of the right ordering of the world, some will take firm stances and prepare for ideological conflict. In this mind-set, it is easy to reframe the world as a place of us versus them. It is possible to unlock some of that defensive posturing by helping students understand that the wide variety of teachings on sexuality that come from religious traditions are not held by monsters and angels in a battle over righteousness but rather that the religious landscape is complicated by human beings who have come to the subject of sexuality with particular sets of presuppositions, assumptions, definitions, personal commitments, and experiences. When students are afforded the opportunity to explore another point of view, they can see why others would hold the positions they do, and they can more charitably talk about the premises of certain arguments and how they hold together. If dialogue on religion and sexuality informs students about different points of view, student affairs professionals and faculty will have, in partnership, encouraged the kind of dialogue that helps students better understand one another, as well as the world in which they live.

References

American College Personnel Association (ACPA). "Student Learning Imperative: Implications for Student Affairs." 1996. Retrieved Dec. 12, 2007, from http://www.myacpa. org/sli_delete/sli.htm.

American Psychological Association. "Answers to Your Questions About Sexual Orientation and Homosexuality." n.d. Retrieved Dec. 12, 2007, from http://www.apa.org/topics/orientation.html.

Biale, R. "Sexuality and Marital Relations." In K. Lebacqz (ed.), *Sexuality: A Reader.* Cleveland, Ohio: Pilgrim Press, 1999.

Farley, M. "Sexual Ethics." In J. Nelson and S. Longfellow (eds.), *Sexuality and the Sacred.* Louisville, Ky.: Westminster/John Knox Press, 1994.

Feray, J. C., and Herzer, M. "Homosexual Studies and Politics in the Nineteenth Century: Karl Maria Kertbeny." *Journal of Homosexuality,* 1990, *19*(1), 23–47.

Nelson, J. *Embodiment.* Minneapolis, Minn.: Augsburg Press, 1978.

Robinson, G. *Essential Judaism.* New York: Pocket Books, 2000.

Sacred Congregation for the Doctrine of the Faith. "Declaration on Certain Questions Concerning Sexual Ethics." Dec. 29, 1975. Retrieved Dec. 12, 2007, from http://www. ourladyswarriors.org/teach/pershuma.htm.

RICHARD W. MCCARTY *is an assistant professor of religious studies at Mercyhurst College in Erie, Pennsylvania.*

6

We provide a brief overview of Muslim college students and the issues they face on campus. Specific practical suggestions are given on what student affairs professionals can do to combat hostility toward Islamic religious groups through the use of dialogue and to create safe spaces for Muslim students to engage in spiritual exploration.

Practical Suggestions to Accommodate the Needs of Muslim Students on Campus

Saba Rasheed Ali, Elham Bagheri

Within higher education, Muslim students face internal and external challenges to adherence to Islam. These students report feeling judged by others because of their religious affiliation (Nasir and Al-Amin, 2006). Many Muslim students report apprehension and discomfort in performing Islamic duties that are visible to the public, including prayer, fasting, modest dress, and nonconsumption of alcohol (Nasir and Al-Amin, 2006). A lack of accommodation for religious practices such as a safe space for prayer, meal accommodations, and acknowledgment of Islamic practices and holidays by administrators and professors can also be problematic for Muslim students (Nasir and Al-Amin, 2006).

Given these challenges, it is important that student affairs practitioners find ways to assist Muslim students in their adherence to their religion as they pursue their degree. In this chapter, we present a brief introduction to Islamic tenets, discuss challenges facing Muslim college students, and offer practical strategies and suggestions for student affairs practitioners to better assist Muslim students. We conclude with a discussion of ways that student affairs practitioners can combat hostility toward the Islamic religion and Muslim students.

NEW DIRECTIONS FOR STUDENT SERVICES, no. 125, Spring 2009   © Wiley Periodicals, Inc.
Published online in Wiley InterScience (www.interscience.wiley.com) • DOI: 10.1002/ss.307

Introduction to Islam

The religion of Islam has an estimated 1 billion followers (called Muslims), making it the second largest religion in the world. Islam is growing in the United States and is soon projected to be the second largest faith group in the country. Currently there are approximately 6 to 8 million Muslims living in the United States (U.S. State Department, 2001). Muslims in the United States are a diverse group and are associated with various racial/ethnic backgrounds, including Arabs (26.2 percent), South Asians (24.7 percent), African Americans (23.8 percent), Caucasian and Native Americans (11 percent), Middle Eastern non-Arabs (10.3 percent), and East Asians (6.4 percent; U.S. State Department, 2001). It is estimated that approximately seventy-five thousand Muslim students are enrolled in American colleges and universities (Rossi, 2002).

Islam is a monotheistic Abrahamic religion. *Islam* means "surrender," and *Muslim* means "one who submits to the will of Allah." Muslims use the word *Allah* to refer to the God of all humanity (Ali, Liu, and Humedian, 2004). The Qur'an is the holy book for Muslims and is believed to be the fundamental source of Islamic principles and values. There are two sects of Islam, Shia and Sunni, which resulted from disagreements in the late seventh century among Muslims regarding the religious and political leadership of the Islamic community. Although there are some differences between the two sects, the core beliefs of Islam are the same for both.

In Islam there are five articles of faith, commonly referred to as the five pillars of Islam: (1) *Iman* or faith (belief in One God), (2) prayer five times daily (*salat*), (3) *zakat* or charity, (4) *sawm* or fasting from sunrise to sunset for thirty days during the month of Ramadan, and (5) *hajj* or a once-in-a-lifetime pilgrimage to Mecca. Although the five pillars are the same for all Muslims, there is a wide variety of nationalities, ethnic backgrounds, and different sects represented within Islam. There are also many differences in terms of the traditions and customs that are followed.

The Context of Islamophobia

In the United States, Islam has tended to be a religion that has not been well understood, and the terrorist attacks of September 11, 2001, resulted in an increase in the marginalization and discrimination of Muslims. The tragedy of 9/11 was unique in that an entire group of individuals, Muslims, were considered the perpetrators and an entire nation, which is majority Christian, was considered the victim. Therefore, the events of 9/11 sparked not only a political conflict but also a theological conflict.

While Islam was misunderstood prior to 9/11, the media coverage of the tragedies focused on the extreme differences between Muslims and Western traditions and religious beliefs. Although Muslims believe Islam is a continuation of Judaism and Christianity, the media and many high-profile evangelical figureheads characterized Islam as a religion that is in considerable conflict with Christianity. In their characterization, they often exacerbated problems in understanding the religion of Islam and brought more attention to a minority of extremists while ignoring the voices of the majority of Muslims who do not adhere to extremist beliefs and behaviors (Takim, 2004).

After September 11, 2001, an increase in Islamophobia became an unfortunate reality for Muslims and those who resembled individuals from Muslim countries (Council on American-Islamic Relations, 2007). The negative beliefs and perceptions about Islam and the Middle East caused individuals to retaliate against those who appeared to be the cause of the terrorist tragedies (Henderson and Sims, 2004). Hate crimes "have consisted of telephone, internet, mail, and face-to-face threats; minor assaults as well as assaults with dangerous weapons and assaults resulting in serious injury and death; and vandalism, shootings, arson and bombings directed at homes, businesses, and places of worship" (U.S. Department of Justice, 2007).

Muslims on College Campuses. Muslims on college campuses are not immune to these personal threats and discrimination in spite of the pretense that most college campuses produce an environment tolerant of differences. Muslim students who have been victims of hate crimes suffer from significant physical, psychological, and emotional consequences. Threat to physical well-being is the most obvious negative consequence of hate crimes for victims; however, there are also significant psychological effects for victims. Victims of hate crimes have been shown to incur long-term posttraumatic stress disorder and need longer to recover from the incident than victims of crimes that were not motivated by bias and hate (Herek, Gillis, Cogan, and Glunt, 1997). Victims of hate crimes may also believe that all individuals who are of the perpetrators' social group hold the same harmful intentions as the perpetrator (Henderson and Sloan, 2003).

Hate Crimes in the Classroom. Hate crimes are one way in which anti-Islamic sentiment has been manifested, but more subtle anti-Islamic sentiment may also be present in the classroom. Universities are hotbeds for debates concerning politics and religion. Many classes are focused exclusively on such topics, and the current political climate can make discussions in the classroom a difficult experience for Muslim students.

Although classroom discussions should be challenging and students have the right to express their beliefs and opinions, if such discussions are not monitored properly by professors, they can lead to the expression of ridicule and discrimination toward Muslims and Islam (Speck, 1997). Muslim students have also reported hesitance in correcting professors due to viewing the professor as an authority figure with power over their grades and class standing (Speck, 1997).

Anti-Islamic sentiment in the classroom can also contribute to feelings of isolation among Muslim students, especially if a student is the only Muslim in the class. The simple fact of being a minority in the classroom can create an uncomfortable learning environment. In classes that discuss social, cultural, and religious topics, the potential for discrimination is always present.

Because Muslim students are typically a minority in classrooms, they often feel obligated to be representatives of their religion and culture (Nasir and Al-Amin, 2006). Representing an entire group of people and feeling responsible for disconfirming stereotypes can be a daunting task for students in the classroom.

Institutional Policies and Barriers to the Practice of Islam

One of the most apparent manifestations of Christian privilege in universities is the academic calendar. It is centered on Christian holidays and fails to recognize holidays of other faiths, including Islam. In Islam there are two holidays that are celebrated by all Muslims and other events that are considered holidays by some Muslims. Because universities in non-Islamic countries, such as the United States, do not officially recognize Islamic holidays, Muslim students struggle with the decision of fulfilling their academic responsibilities or observing their religious holidays. Such a decision can be a stressful and difficult experience for Muslim students who value both their academic obligations and their religious duties.

Another institutional barrier for practicing Islam on college campuses is lack of a safe space for prayer (Blumenfeld, 2006). Islamic prayer is a ritual that needs to be conducted five times a day at specific times. When safe and established places are not available, Muslim students have reported discomfort and anxiety from searching for a place to pray on campus (Nasir and Al-Amin, 2006). They feel that other students and faculty do not understand the process of Islamic prayer, and this makes praying in public spaces an uncomfortable experience for them (Nasir and Al-Amin, 2006). Another barrier to conducting prayer is when academic obligations, such as class or meetings, overlap with prayer times (Speck, 1997).

Dietary Restrictions. In Islam there are certain dietary restrictions that some Muslims strictly follow while others may not. These include the consumption of halal meat, which is slaughtered in the name of God, and prohibition against eating pork. For Muslim students who do adhere to the dietary restrictions, dining options on college campuses may not be adequate. Dining availability also becomes an issue for Muslim students during the month of Ramadan when they fast from sunrise to sunset, and dining hall schedules may not be accommodating.

Islam forbids the consumption of alcohol. Given that a source of entertainment on college campuses involves drinking, Muslims may feel socially isolated from their peers. They may also have very few choices in entertainment and social outlets.

NEW DIRECTIONS FOR STUDENT SERVICES • DOI: 10.1002/ss

Female Muslim Students. Female Muslim students may need additional support because of the issues they face in terms of cultural expectations and discrimination experiences. These students may need safe spaces to discuss their concerns about religious practice. An issue of particular significance for Muslim women on college campuses is that of choosing to wear the hijab (veil). There is not one universally accepted definition of hijab in Islam, which is why women who choose to wear the hijab may look different depending on their nationality and culture. In most instances, the hijab involves covering the hair with a veil and modest dress that covers most of the body.

Student affairs practitioners may be able to establish support groups for Muslim women who are struggling with issues concerning hijab, especially in dormitories or other student housing facilities. These groups may be able to bring together women from across campus to help them negotiate their religious identity and the ways in which they choose to express it. It may also strengthen their ability to provide information about this practice to the non-Muslim community.

Practical Suggestions

Student affairs practitioners can assist Muslim students in overcoming barriers to spiritual exploration and religious adherence in many ways. In addition, they can be instrumental in improving campus climate for Muslim students by directly addressing Islamaphobia and misunderstandings between Muslim and non-Muslim students. We provide strategies for improving Muslim students' experiences, as well as the campus climate:

- One simple way that universities can create a climate conducive to religious adherence among Muslims students is to include Islamic religious holidays on the academic calendar. Although the holidays may not be officially recognized by the university, an alternate calendar with a description of the holidays can educate faculty and administrators on this topic. It is important that faculty and administrators show public support for Muslim students.
- Student affairs practitioners can create safe places for Muslim students to pray and hold services. Campuses across the United States have created student centers or provided available spaces to Muslim students for the purpose of religious gatherings and prayer (Eckstrom, 2000). Muslim students have found this to be a significant sign of support on behalf of their college community (Eckstrom, 2000) that leads to an improvement in morale and communicates to non-Muslim students an appreciation for religious diversity. It is also important to provide adequate accommodations for students to pray during the required prayer time. One way this might be accomplished is for college student practitioners to survey Muslim students on campus in order to investigate their specific needs for accommodation (Speck, 1997).

- Evaluate dining options and consider whether the dietary needs of Muslim students are being met. Dining hall accommodations include providing adequate nonpork meals, providing halal meat (kosher meat is acceptable), and adjusting the schedule during the month of Ramadan.
- Set up alcohol-free social experiences that might not only benefit Muslim students but attract other students who do not drink alcohol. A side benefit may be promotion of commonalities between Muslim students and other students who choose not to drink.
- Organize panel discussions and educational opportunities that open up for discussion the role of women in Islam and the role of hijab to help clear up misunderstandings and correct misinformation. Allowing non-Muslims to ask questions without fear of evaluation or defensiveness may directly address the concerns and biases that non-Muslim students have about the practice of hijab.

The following suggestions can assist student affairs practitioners to foster better relations among Muslim and non-Muslim students:

- Work directly with Muslim student associations to provide information to non-Muslim students. Panels and guest speakers are ways of providing information. However, simple exposure through social experiences may also go a long way in promoting an appreciation for diversity. Social experiences centered around the Islamic holidays can be organized in collaboration with these associations. These celebrations could be fun experiences that increase the casual contact of people of different faiths and improve relations between Muslim and non-Muslim groups.
- Sponsor a "fast for a day" event during the month of Ramadan in which students are encouraged to refrain from drinking and eating from sunrise to sunset for one day (this is the fasting that Muslims practice during the thirty-day period of Ramadan). After sunset, sponsor an *iftar,* the traditional evening meal for breaking the daily fast. *Iftar* is often done as a community, with Muslims gathering to break their fast together. The sponsorship of this event promotes an understanding of Islam and the practice of fasting that extends beyond lectures and panel discussions to promote an actual experience for non-Muslim students.
- Create safe dialogue. Most college campuses strive to educate students and encourage critical thinking about global and local events. Given the current political climate and world events, heated discussions about political issues that are intertwined with religious conflicts may be inevitable. These discussions, if not carefully handled, can lead to increased hostility between Muslim and non-Muslim students. Therefore, it is important to provide safe spaces for these discussions and ensure they are properly mediated.
- Train professors to manage difficult political and religious disagreements in class, especially classes where group discussion participation is one facet of grading criteria. Training should address educating faculty in how

to mediate discussions between Muslim and non-Muslim students and how to implement appropriate strategies to include Muslim students who may feel alienated in classroom discussions. These trainings can be offered through centers for teaching or international services.

* Dialogue and collaboration between Muslims and non-Muslims can be facilitated through student organizations. For example, encouraging various religious communities to participate in interfaith dialogues and social service projects can spark common ground between Muslims and other religious communities. Interfaith service projects in which two or more faith groups collaborate on a community-enhancing project are being practiced in a variety of settings and often take people from different religious backgrounds beyond discussions into social action. These interfaith groups can also serve as a safe space for Muslim students to find support and allies outside their own faith community.

Conclusion

Fostering a multicultural environment must be a priority for college campuses as their campuses become more diverse. In particular, with the current political and social climate, multicultural awareness surrounding Islam and the experiences of Muslim students has become increasingly important. Raising awareness and increasing knowledge is the first step; however, taking action is the most effective means by which campuses can become advocates for Muslim students. It is action that will provide evidence that the campus is committed to creating an environment that not only acknowledges and appreciates the diversity that Muslim students contribute to campus, but is also dedicated to ensuring that Muslim students are recognized as valued members of the campus community.

References

Ali S. R., Liu, W. and Humedian, M. "Islam 101: Understanding the Religion and Therapy Implications." *Professional Psychology: Research and Practice,* 2004, *35,* 635–642.

Blumenfeld, W. J. "Christian Privilege and the Promotion of 'Secular' and Not-So 'Secular' Mainline Christianity in Schooling and the Larger Society." *Equity and Excellence in Education,* 2006, *39,* 195–210.

Council on American-Islamic Relations. "Islamophobia." 2007. Retrieved Jan. 15, 2007, from www.cair.com/Issues/Islamophobia/Islamophobia.aspx.

Eckstrom, K. "More Colleges Becoming Muslim Friendly." *Staten Island Advance,* Apr. 8, 2000.

Henderson, K. C., and Sims, M. B. "An Investigation of African American College Students' Beliefs About Anti–Middle Eastern Hate Crime and Victims in the Wake of September 11th." *Western Journal of Black Studies,* 2004, *28,* 511–517.

Henderson, K. C., and Sloan, R. "After the Hate: Helping Psychologists Help Victims of Racist Hate Crime." *Clinical Psychology: Science and Practice,* 2003, *10,* 481–490.

Herek, G. M., Gillis, J. R., Cogan, J. C., and Glunt, E. K. "Hate Crime Victimization Among Lesbian, Gay, and Bisexual Adults: Prevalence, Psychological Correlates and Methodological Issues." *Journal of Interpersonal Violence,* 1997, *12,* 195–215.

Nasir, N. S., and Al-Amin, J. "Creating Identity-Safe Spaces on College Campuses for Muslim Students." *Change*, 2006, 22–27.

Rossi, H. L. "Muslim Chaplains a New Priority for College Campuses." Pew Forum for Religion and Public Life. 2002. Retrieved Jan. 10, 2007, from http://pewforum.org/news/display.php?NewsID=1203.

Speck, B. W. "Respect for Religious Difference: The Case of Muslim Students." In D. L. Sigsbee, B. W. Speck, and B. Maylath (eds.), *Approaches to Teaching Non-Native English Speakers Across the Curriculum*. New Directions for Teaching and Learning, no. 70. San Francisco: Jossey-Bass, 1997.

Suad, N., and Al-Amin, J. "Creating Identity-Safe Spaces on College Campuses for Muslim Students." *Change*, 2006, 22–27.

Takim, L. (2004). "From Conversion to Conversation: Interfaith Dialogue in Post 9–11 America." *Muslim World*, 2004, *94*, 343–355.

U.S. Department of Justice. "Post 9/11 Activity Update." Enforcement and Outreach Following the September 11 Terrorist Attacks, 1997. Retrieved Jan. 10, 2007, from http://www.usdoj.gov/crt/legalinfo/discrimupdate.htm.

U.S. State Department. *Fact Sheet: Islam in the United States*. 2001. Retrieved December, 12, 2001, from http://uninfo.state.gove/usa/islam/fact2.htm.

SABA RASHEED ALI *is an assistant professor of counseling psychology in the Department of Psychological and Quantitative Foundations at the University of Iowa.*

ELHAM BAGHERI *is a doctoral student in the counseling psychology program in the Department of Psychological and Quantitative Foundations at the University of Iowa.*

7

*This chapter describes atheism in higher education and
provides suggestions for student affairs practitioners
interested in understanding and responding to the needs
of atheist students.*

Invisible, Marginalized, and Stigmatized: Understanding and Addressing the Needs of Atheist Students

Kathleen M. Goodman, John A. Mueller

Atheist students, like atheists in the broader society, are often stigmatized as immoral, evil, or god hating. Because of this stigmatization, it is common for atheists to hide that aspect of their identity, rendering them invisible. Educators contribute to that invisibility when they fail to include non-believing perspectives in religious and spiritual development work with students, thus marginalizing atheist students further. We encourage educators to learn about atheism and make efforts to normalize it, while seeking ways to provide developmental opportunities for atheist students.

Historically, the student affairs profession has been dedicated to the holistic development of all students (American Council on Education, 2004; NASPA, n.d.). Student affairs practitioners create developmental spaces for all types of students while educating the "majority" about multiculturalism, sexual orientation, nontraditional students, and students of diverse religious backgrounds. These practitioners are guided by a dedication to the whole student, to serving every student, and to "education for a fuller realization of democracy" (NASPA, n.d.). Yet as this chapter demonstrates, the needs of atheist students have generally been ignored by the profession.

In this chapter, we introduce the topic of atheist students to the field of student affairs. We provide definitions of relevant terms related to the

perspectives and principles of atheists. Then we briefly address the demographics of atheism and focus on atheist student experiences on college campuses. We conclude with recommendations for student affairs practitioners.

Defining and Understanding Atheism

Smith (1979) offers a cogent examination of the terms *theism, atheism,* and *agnosticism.* Smith defines *theism* as "belief in a god or gods" (p. 9). Since the prefix "a" means "without," *atheism* then means "without a belief in a god or gods." Baggini (2003) and Converse (2003) argue that atheism is not only the absence of belief in god's existence, but a complete denial of anything supernatural. Whereas theism and atheism are concerned with different aspects of religious belief, agnosticism, according to Smith (1979), refers to "the impossibility of knowledge with regard to a god" (p. 10). Atheist students come to campus informed by these definitions and others. How they define atheism and identify themselves inevitably affects how they live.

Converse (2003) differentiates among three types of atheists based on how they express their nonbelief in their lives. The first type, and arguably the most common, accepts that god does not exist, but does not give much thought to that position and has difficulty justifying it. They simply, from Dawkins's perspective (2006), live their lives on the assumption that god is not there. The second type accepts the position that god does not exist and can offer an articulate statement on that position, incorporating knowledge from religion, science, and technology. The third type differs from the second in a willingness to both publicly take a stance on and structure life around atheism. Atheist students hold these varying perspectives as well, and many need help sorting out their beliefs and articulating their identity.

A number of other terms identify people who are atheists, such as *nonbeliever, secular humanist, naturalist,* and *freethinker.* It is beyond the scope of this chapter to examine each of these terms and the many reasons that people adopt them. However, one possible explanation may lie in the stigma associated with the term *atheism,* which is often characterized as a dark force that rejects the values of goodness, ethics, morality, and purpose. Atheist scholars point out that nonbelievers can live a moral life independent of a god in large part because the atheist is less likely than the believer to confuse divine law and selected scriptural text with what is fundamentally right, just, and good for the sake of humankind (Baggini, 2003; Comte-Sponville, 2007; Paulos, 2008; Stenger, 2007). Likewise, these scholars assert that atheists can live with meaning and direction, not for the purpose of a creator, but for themselves, humanity, and the earth. Indeed, many nonbelieving students view their atheism as more than a rejection of religion; it is their life philosophy that provides moral direction (Nussbaum, 1999).

NEW DIRECTIONS FOR STUDENT SERVICES • DOI: 10.1002/ss

Demographics

It is difficult to obtain an accurate set of demographics on atheists for two reasons. First, a single definition and identity of an atheist is not universally accepted or understood and is often not distinguished from *agnostic, nonreligious,* or *secularist.* Second, and related to terminology, the social stigma attached with the term *atheist* results in many not reporting themselves as atheist on surveys. Still, some data provide an idea of the demographics of atheists.

The *Encyclopedia Britannica* (2004) reported that 12.5 percent of the world's population is nonreligious, and 2.4 percent are atheist. This is substantiated by estimates from a 2002 survey by Adherents.com (n.d.) that reported 14 percent of the world's population as secular, nonreligious, agnostic, or atheist. *U.S. News and World Report* cites a Harris Poll that found an increase in the number of adult Americans who were not "absolutely certain" about the existence of God from 34 percent to 43 percent over three years (Tolson, 2006). Still, a study by the University of Minnesota sociology department (Edgell, Gerteis and Hartmann, 2006) reports that self-reported atheists account for only about 1 to 3 percent of the U.S. population.

This same study found that atheists are the least trusted segment of the population, ranking below Muslims, recent immigrants, and gays and lesbians (Edgell, Gerteis, and Hartmann, 2006). The authors suggest that not sharing in the American core value of religion is what marginalizes atheists so dramatically. The study also reports that in addition to personal religiosity, exposure to diversity, education, and political orientation influences attitudes toward atheists.

Atheism in Higher Education

According to the 2003 Higher Education Research Institute (HERI) study, *The Spiritual Life of College Students* (2004–2005), 17 percent of students surveyed picked "none" as their stated religious preference, and 15 percent stated that they were not interested in "spiritual/religious matters" (p. 6). However, practically no research exists to shed light on the experience of atheist college students (Nash, 2003). This gap suggests that, like atheists in the general population, atheists on campus are invisible, stigmatized, and marginalized. Anecdotal evidence supports this claim.

Reflecting on his experience teaching religious studies classes on religion, Nash (2003) states that many atheist students feel stigmatized and demonized. He provides evidence from one graduate student who asked, "Where is the acceptance of non-believers? When will atheists like myself feel that it is safe to state our ideas . . . ?" (p. 1). Nash attributes stigmatization to atheophobia, which he defines as "the fear and loathing of atheists that permeate American culture" (p. 4). This is also expressed by a Harvard undergraduate and atheist student leader who states that even on a tolerant campus like Harvard, he meets people who "despise" him for his beliefs (Reisberg, 1998, para. 29).

Atheophobia leads to invisibility for many atheists, who find it is best to keep their nonbelief hidden for their own good. In one telling example, Pollit (2005) describes the case of Tim Shortell, a professor being considered for a department chair position at Brooklyn College of the City University of New York until the local newspapers identified him as an atheist. The college president instituted an investigation, and Shortell ultimately withdrew his candidacy, forgoing a professional opportunity because his nonbelief was made visible. Likewise, Nash (2003) reflects that it is unlikely that an individual who is open about being an atheist would be hired as a president of a prestigious college or university.

Contributing to the invisibility and marginalization of atheist students is the current focus on religious pluralism and spirituality on campus (Nussbaum, 1999; Nash, 2003; Goodman and Teraguchi, 2008). Rarely do educators include nonbelieving worldviews when addressing religious diversity. While *spirituality* is considered an inclusive term, it has different meanings to different people and is not a relevant concept for all students, as the HERI data indicate (2004–2005). As long as student affairs educators continue to use spiritual (Love and Talbot, 2000) and faith development models (Parks, 2000) that assume students believe in a higher power of some sort, the atheist perspective will continue to be marginalized. As long as student affairs educators continue to ignore nonbelieving perspectives, atheist students will remain invisible. And as long student affairs educators allow the persistence of myths and misconceptions about atheists living amoral and meaningless lives, atheist students will continue to be stigmatized.

Offering a positive counter to the invisibility and stigmatization of atheist college students is the Campus Freethought Alliance (CFA), a national organization that supports individual student organizations of nonbelievers (Nussbaum, 1999; Reisberg, 1998). The goal of the campus organizations is to create a sense of community among nonbelievers. They serve a function similar to Hillel, Campus Crusade for Christ, and other religious groups, providing students the opportunity to develop community, host lectures, and become activists on their own behalf (Nussbaum, 1999). CFA also provides students with an opportunity to develop their moral beliefs and discuss how they make meaning in their lives (Nussbaum, 1999). Many of the students, like other atheists and secular humanists, "find meaning and moral guidance through scientific reasoning, the lessons of history, and personal experiences" (Reisberg, 1998, para. 9).

Suggestions for Student Affairs Practice

Atheist students are often marginalized by higher education professionals, knowingly or unknowingly, to the point of being made to feel invisible on college campuses. This condition creates a unique challenge to student affairs practitioners who may genuinely want to respond to the needs of this

NEW DIRECTIONS FOR STUDENT SERVICES • DOI: 10.1002/ss

population. We propose the following recommendations to assist practitioners in understanding and responding to the needs of atheist students:

- *Learn about and understand atheism.* "Atheophobia, like all other phobias,
  thrives in a state of ignorance" (Nash, 2003, p. 7), and higher education
  professionals know as well as anyone else that knowledge and education can go a long way in combating fear, dismantling stereotypes, and
  replacing misinformation with accurate information. Therefore, professionals need to take time to learn more about atheism, including its history and
  principles, as well as related myths and misconceptions. This knowledge
  can undergird and advance the other recommendations in this section. The
  references in this chapter, along with the Web site www.atheists.org, provide a useful starting point for increasing one's knowledge about atheism.
- *Assess your campus climate for atheist students.* Conduct a formal or informal assessment of your campus climate for nonbelievers. The following
  questions can guide such assessments:

  - Does your campus provide sufficient opportunities for inner develop-
    ment independent of religion?
  - Do forums for religious inquiry value the many differences within and
    between religious traditions and include nonreligious and nonbeliev-
    ing perspectives?
  - Have the faculty and administrators on your campus grappled with the
    definitions of spirituality and religion and the ways that their diverse
    meanings may affect students?
  - Have you analyzed the impact of Christian and religious privilege on
    your campus?
  - Are there sufficient opportunities for nonbelievers to come together for
    community and support?

Formal assessments can include specific campus surveys on tolerance of
religious belief and nonbelief, or these types of items can be added to existing campus climate surveys.

- *Normalize the atheist perspective.* Student affairs practitioners can help
  reduce the invisibility and stigmatization of atheist students by openly talking about atheism and providing information to the campus. The presence
  of programming opportunities about atheism or targeted for atheist students
  can make the topic visible and valid. Many of the other recommendations
  in this section can also contribute to normalizing atheism on campus.
- *Challenge the tacit definition of and ways of thinking about spirituality.* Challenge the idea that spirituality is a one-size-fits-all concept by acknowledging atheist perspectives in all campus efforts on spirituality. This may mean
  being very intentional about expanding the concept of spirituality to

include atheism. Or it may mean letting go of the word *spirituality* in favor of *inner development, existential well-being,* or *life purpose and meaning.*

- *Include atheist students in programming.* In efforts to promote spirituality (or inner development) of students, be inclusive of atheist students. Offer opportunities for personal development that ring true for atheist students; they are as eager as other students to explore what they believe and how their beliefs influence their identity, purpose, morality, and ethics. Consider providing opportunities for discussion in a safe setting of atheists only. Also, consider how inner development, belief, and nonbelief can be incorporated into other program topics, such as leadership development. Just as educators encourage students to learn about, respect, and appreciate different religious (theist and polytheist) perspectives, so too can they encourage students to understand and not feel threatened by the nonreligious or atheist perspectives. Finally, invite atheist speakers to campus, using the speakers' bureau maintained by the American Atheists (http://www. atheists.org/visitors.center/speakers.html). All of these programming opportunities allow atheist and theist students to discuss how they develop values, how they find meaning in life, and how to build community.

- *Be aware of sources of marginalization.* Many times, atheists feel marginalized by traditions and practices that other people take for granted. One way to address this is to be conscious of the presence of atheist students on campuses and to examine practices that assume students' comfort with religious-based practices. For example, many formal activities on campuses, such as commencements, use invocations or benedictions that connote religion (typically Christian), even when attempts are made to be secular. This marginalization can even find its way into our casual language. Paulos (2008) notes that many common sayings can be rephrased without references to god. For example, "God only knows" essentially means, "No one really knows," and "God willing" implies "If things work out ok" (p. 136).

- *Include the atheist perspective in campus interfaith efforts.* Cawthon and Jones (2004) observed that in the past two decades, and in response to students' increasing search for spiritual growth, there has been a resurgence of campus exploration on church and institutional relations. This is particularly evident in campus ministry programs and interfaith councils. We urge student affairs divisions to collaborate to find ways to make nonbelief more visible within faith communities, campus ministries, and interfaith councils. This may even include the bold step of creating a chaplaincy for nonbelievers, such as Harvard University's humanist chaplaincy, which is "dedicated to building, educating, and nurturing a diverse community of humanists, agnostics, atheists, and the non-religious at Harvard and beyond" (http://www.harvardhumanist.org/).

- *Build a visible network of atheist allies among faculty and staff.* Given the demographics of atheists and agnostics, it is reasonable to assume there are higher education professionals who are nonbelievers or are questioning the existence of god. Similarly, there are likely to be theists whose knowledge about and openness to atheism qualifies them as allies. We suggest that student affairs practitioners identify and build this network of allies to provide support for programs, campus assessments, and formal ally groups for students. To take this further, perhaps initiate a program similar to Safe Zone programs for gay, lesbian, bisexual, and transgender students.

- *Disseminate information about scholarships for atheist students.* Campuses often make available to students a wide range of scholarships (usually through announcements or institutional websites dedicated to that topic). Educators are encouraged to provide information about atheist scholarships directly to atheist students and to include it with other scholarship notices. American Atheists provides scholarships of up to two thousand dollars for atheist activism (http://www.atheists.org/family/html/scholarship.html).

- *Help students connect to a broader atheist community using technology.* The Internet has become an important source of information and social networking for students in general, and in particular for students who feel stigmatized or desire to maintain anonymity. We urge practitioners to use the Internet and other forms of technology to help connect atheist students to one another and the larger atheist community. Information for using Facebook in this way can be found at http://friendlyatheist.com/2007/08/22/how-to-use-facebook-to-your-advantage/. In addition, the Atheist Blogroll (http://friendlyatheist.com/blogroll/) provides links to multiple online groups.

- *Encourage the formation of an atheist student organization.* If your campus has a group for atheist students, get involved or at least become aware of its presence, leadership, mission, and meeting times. If no such group exists, encourage its formation or help to found one by using information from the Campus Freethought Alliance (http://www.campusfreethought.org/) or the Secular Student Alliance (www.secularstudents.org).

- *Conduct research.* The previous recommendations for practice have the potential to significantly minimize the invisibility and stigmatization of atheist students. Likewise, research on the lives, experiences, and development of this population can facilitate this objective. As noted earlier, very little is known or understood about atheist students. Still, as many are aware from theories of faith development (Fowler, 1981; Parks, 2000), the college-age years are a significant time for testing and questioning one's faith. Arguably, then, the college years might become a starting point for some young adults who, in their search for meaning, purpose, beliefs, and attitudes, develop an atheist perspective. There is much to learn about atheist students in pursuit of making the campus more open and hospitable for them.

- *Resist the temptation to wait for a critical mass.* We suggest that given student affairs professional philosophy and goals, it is imprudent (and perhaps unethical) to fail to respond to the existence and the needs of this student population. Like other invisible or underrepresented minorities, it may be difficult to assess their presence on campus, but that does not mean they do not exist. Just as we have not waited for other religious minorities, such as Buddhists and Muslims, or gender minorities, such as transgender people, to reach a critical mass before acknowledging and responding to their presence on campus, we should not wait for atheist students.

Conclusion

The information in this chapter is a starting point for student affairs practitioners to understand atheism and begin to create the safe, affirming campus climates that they profess to desire. The tips for practice should help practitioners reduce the invisibility, marginalization, and stigmatization of atheist students. Student affairs practitioners can normalize atheism and begin to address the needs of atheist students by creating inclusive dialogues about religion, spirituality, belief, and nonbelief. As Nash (2003) reminds us, this type of dialogue "requires direct, give-and-take participation with all types of religious otherness, including non-religious otherness. It insists that we allow the 'other' to get under our skins, to engage with us, to disturb us, and even, if the circumstances warrant, to *change* us" (p. 19).

References

Adherents.com. "Major Religions of the World Ranked by Number of Adherents." N.d. Retrieved Jan. 2, 2008, from http://adherents.com/Religions_By_Adherents.html.

American Council on Education. "The Student Personnel Point of View (1937)." In E. J. Whitt (ed.), *ASHE Reader on College Student Affairs Administration*. Boston: Pearson Custom, 2004.

Baggini, J. *Atheism: A Very Short Introduction*. New York: Oxford University Press, 2003.

Cawthon, T. W., and Jones, C. "A Description of Traditional and Contemporary Campus Ministries." *College Student Affairs Journal*, 2004, 23, 158–172.

Comte-Sponville, A. *The Little Book of Atheist Spirituality*. (N. Huston, Trans.). New York: Viking/Penguin Group, 2007. (Original work published in 2006)

Converse, R. W. *Atheism as a Positive Social Force*. New York: Algora, 2003.

Dawkins, R. *The God Delusion*. Boston: Houghton Mifflin, 2006.

Edgell, P., Gerteis, J., and Hartmann, D. "Atheists as 'Other': Moral Boundaries and Cultural Membership in American Society." *American Sociological Review*, 2006, 71, 211–234.

Encyclopedia Britannica. "Worldwide Adherents of All Religions by Six Continental Areas." 2004. Retrieved Jan. 2, 2008, from http://www.britannica.com/eb/article 9396555/Religion.

Fowler, J. W. *Stages of Faith: The Psychology of Human Development and the Quest for Meaning*. San Francisco: HarperCollins, 1981.

Goodman, K. M., and Teraguchi, D. H. "Beyond Spirituality: A New Framework for Educators." *Diversity and Democracy*, 2008, 11(1), 10–11.

Higher Education Research Institute. "The Spiritual Life of College Students: A National Study of College Students' Search for Meaning and Purpose." 2004–2005. Retrieved Oct. 17, 2007, from http://www.spirituality.ucla.edu/reports/index.html

Love, P., and Talbot, D. "Defining Spiritual Development: A Missing Consideration for Student Affairs." *NASPA Journal*, 2000, *37*(1), 361–375.

Nash, R. J. *Religious Pluralism in the Academy: Opening the Dialogue.* New York: Peter Lang, 2001.

Nash, R. J. "Inviting Atheists to the Table: A Modest Proposal for Higher Education." *Religion and Education*, 2003, *30*(1), 1–23.

NASPA. "The Student Personnel Point of View, 1949." N.d. Retrieved Apr. 2, 2007, from http://www.naspa.org/pubs/StudAff_1949.pdf.

Nussbaum, E. "Faith No More: The Campus Crusade for Secular Humanism." *Lingua Franca*, 1999, *9*(7), 30–37.

Parks, S. D. *Big Questions, Worthy Dreams: Mentoring Young Adults in Their Search for Meaning, Purpose, and Faith.* San Francisco: Jossey-Bass, 2000.

Paulos, J. A. *Irreligion: A Mathematician Explains Why the Arguments for God Just Don't Add Up.* New York: Hill and Wang, 2008.

Pollit, K. "Brooklyn Prof in Godless Shocker." *Nation*, June 27, 2005, p. 11.

Reisberg, L. "New Groups Unite in Belief That One Needn't Believe in God." *Chronicle of Higher Education*, 1998, *44*(32), pp. A43–44.

Smith, G. H. *Atheism: The Case Against God.* Buffalo, N.Y.: Prometheus Books, 1979.

Stenger, V. J. *God: The Failed Hypothesis—How Science Shows That God Does Not Exist.* New York: Prometheus Books, 2007.

Tolson, J. "The New Unbelievers." *U.S. News and World Report*, Nov. 13, 2006, p. 40.

KATHLEEN M. GOODMAN *is a doctoral student and research assistant at the Center for Research on Undergraduate Education at the University of Iowa.*

JOHN A. MUELLER *is an associate professor of student affairs in higher education at Indiana University of Pennsylvania.*

This chapter discusses ways student affairs professionals can use the privileged identity exploration model to facilitate difficult discussions at the intersections of religious privilege. Examples are given and practical suggestions offered on ways to create conditions for productive dialogue.

Facilitating Difficult Dialogues at the Intersections of Religious Privilege

Sherry K. Watt

A core definition of a *difficult dialogue* is a verbal or written exchange of ideas or opinions among citizens within a community that centers on an awakening of potentially conflicting views about beliefs and values (Watt, 2007). As informed by Fried's definition of religious privilege (2007), difficult dialogue at the intersections of religious privilege happens in situations where dominant worldviews (nonsecular values, beliefs, and practices) are unconsciously accepted as the norm and where any secular or nondominant belief systems (Islam, Judaism, atheism) are marginalized. The purpose of this chapter is to discuss the conditions that make dialogue surrounding religious privilege difficult and to share examples of practical ways conversation can be made more productive around these issues.

Elements of Difficult Dialogues

Difficult dialogues at the intersections of religious privilege have at least three elements that create a perfect storm: the juxtaposition of dominant and marginalized groups, the complexity of paradox and polarities, and the affiliation with personal and social identity.

Dominant and Marginalized Paradigm. A contributing factor to difficult dialogues regarding religion is the tension between dominant and marginalized worldview (Goodman, 2001). This paradigm is born out of a complex history where certain groups have been dominant (whites and

NEW DIRECTIONS FOR STUDENT SERVICES, no. 125, Spring 2009   © Wiley Periodicals, Inc.
Published online in Wiley InterScience (www.interscience.wiley.com) • DOI: 10.1002/ss.309

Christians) over others (people of color and Jews). Paulo Freire (1970) first referred to the concept *critical consciousness*. It can be described as the ability to evaluate and take action against the oppressive social, political, and economic elements in a society. Examining religious privilege and the assumptions behind it helps to illuminate the dominant and marginalized social structure that creates oppressive conditions for those who are practicing nonsecular or nondominant belief systems (Seifert, 2007). Encouraging students to discuss the dynamics of power, privilege, and oppression can be extremely challenging for them both emotionally and intellectually. Ultimately, though, this type of challenge will inspire students to take action to change societal injustice.

Paradox and Polarities. Johnson (1996) proposes viewing issues we face as polarities to manage rather than problems to solve. He distinguishes the difference between paradox/polarities and problems in two ways. First, the difficulty associated with the issue is ongoing. Problems have solutions and an end point in the process. Paradoxes are continually in process of solving, and there is no clear end point. Second, within the issue there are two poles that are interdependent. Paradoxes cannot stand alone and depend on the balancing of both ends. In other words, "both one pole and its apparent opposite depend on each other" (p. 82). For instance, discussing atheism presents a paradox or polarity. In a society dominated by theistic belief systems, considering what it means to hold simultaneously the ideals of the dominant Christian belief system in America and at the same time associating that atheists can have morals and be ethical without worshiping a god is quite a paradox. According to Johnson's definition, this dilemma is not a problem because it is not transient. It is a classic issue that entangles the American value of freedom of religion and respect for independence with the predominant charge in being a Christian that says to bring all souls to Christ. Having students grapple with these ideals can spawn personal and social exploration about values, religious practices, and American society that are many-sided. These types of many-sided discussions are common when discussing religious privileges.

Personal and Social Identity. Historically, religion has been a central socializing factor for young children in the United States (Reason and Davis, 2005). Our academic and social calendars have long been designed in such ways that afford time to spend with family during Christian religious holidays (Seifert, 2007). Therefore, our personal and social identities are developed based on expectations that are influenced in this society by religion, most often Christianity. Connections to religion go beyond rituals and doctrine and into the culture of communities and families. Exploring religious privilege often leads to deeply emotional discussions as students consider what it means to leave the security of their socialization that is insulated and reinforced by a regular routine of holiday and family time.

NEW DIRECTIONS FOR STUDENT SERVICES • DOI: 10.1002/ss

The Privileged Identity Exploration Model: Potential Responses for Facilitators

The three elements of dominant/marginalized paradigm, paradox/polarities, and personal/social identity create the perfect storm for dialogue fraught with opportunities for students to present defenses to protect their personal and social identities. The privileged identity exploration (PIE) model identifies eight defenses that students often display when exploring their social or political position in society (Watt, 2007). This section suggests ways student affairs professionals can respond when students are displaying certain defenses in dialogues surrounded by religious privilege and practical suggestions on what practitioners can do to create conditions for productive dialogue.

Using the Privileged Identity Exploration Model: Potential Responses for Facilitators

The Watt (2007) privileged identity exploration (PIE) model sets out eight defensive behaviors students might display when engaging in difficult dialogue. The eight defense modes are categorized by behaviors one exhibits when recognizing, contemplating, or addressing a privileged identity (see Figure 8.1). Recognizing Privilege Identity describes reactions when students initially are presented with anxiety-provoking stimuli surrounding a privileged identity such as their religion. Reactions are denial, deflection, or rationalization. Contemplating Privileged Identity explains individuals' reactions when they are beginning to think more carefully about provoking ideas about a social justice issue, including religion in society, and they may display intellectualization, principium, or false envy defenses. Addressing Privileged Identity portrays behaviors of individuals who are attending to their dissonant feelings about social injustice related to this new awareness, and are involved in some action to resolve the issue. Reactions may be displayed in the defenses of benevolence or minimization.

There are six assumptions underlying the model, two of them particularly relevant to discussions regarding religious privilege: "(1) Engaging in difficult dialogue is a necessary part of unlearning social oppression and (2) Defense modes are normal human reactions to the uncertainty that one feels when exploring their privileged identities in more depth" (Watt, 2007, p. 119). The model assumes that dialogue that creates feelings of discomfort is a normal and necessary part of gaining critical consciousness.

The next sections present brief descriptions of the three defenses (principium, false envy, and benevolence) that are most likely to appear during discussions surrounding religious privilege. Examples are given of potential responses that facilitators can use to avoid allowing the defensive behavior to derail the discussion and instead focus so that individuals can move toward greater critical consciousness. These examples are not intended to be a recipe

NEW DIRECTIONS FOR STUDENT SERVICES • DOI: 10.1002/ss

Figure 8.1. The Privileged Identity Exploration Model

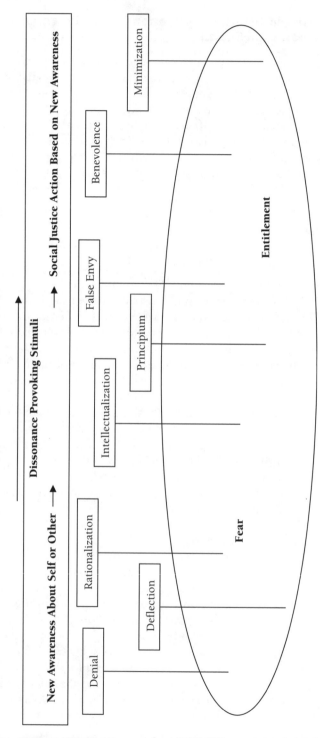

for cross-cultural interactions, but simply suggestions that are meant to be expanded on and personalized to the style of the facilitator.

Principium Potential Responses. A principium response is a defensive reaction driven by a personal or political belief. For example, a student might respond:

> I feel badly for my friend who is a lesbian and the hatred directed toward her. I think that homosexuals have every right that heterosexuals have to love and to be loved in return. However, I feel that God did not intend for men and men or women and women to be together. I believe that marriage is a sacrament intended to unite man and woman through God. I do not think that it is ignorant or intolerant, just what I believe. I do not accept that part of her.

As a facilitator, you want to avoid having the conversation shut down by the trump card of religious beliefs that prevents exploring this issue in any depth. In general, consider how you can give and take in the conversation. For instance, you may need to acknowledge the paradox in the social and political climate that brands this student intolerant in a society where religious freedom is a foundational value, but also have this student sit with the discomfort she is feeling in the moment. You can do this by focusing the conversation on feelings rather than thoughts, values, or beliefs. Explore the feelings of being upset and disheartened. Focus on what it means to experience injustice on a personal and political level. You may want to have her examine the hurt that exists in her friendship and point out comparative types of pain inherent in other social injustices done in this society. You may want to point out injustices that she can relate to that might help her examine her feelings outside this principle. Another option for facilitators might be to ask a what-if question, which attempts to hold in place the arguments about homosexuality and encourage the student to explore in more depth the complexities of the issues facing sexual minorities. For example, you can ask the student: "What if the belief that homosexuality is wrong were set aside as not a right-or-wrong issue for a moment? How then would you view rights and privileges for same-sex marriage?" Exploring this question and subsequent others might lead the student toward raising her critical consciousness by exploring Christian privilege and how the social and political structure in this society supports homoprejudice (Logan, 1996).

False Envy Potential Responses. A false envy defense is signified by a display of affection for a person or a feature of a person in an effort to deny the complexity of the social and political context. In a discussion examining issues related to Muslims and race, a student displaying a false envy defense might say:

> I do not know many Muslim women. I have noticed that some wear the hijab, and some do not. I expect to see Middle Eastern women wearing it, but not African American Muslims. It makes me uncomfortable for the African

American woman because I think she might be associated with the Nation of Islam and that radical thinking. I associate Middle Eastern women wearing hijabs with being married to a man who oppresses her. What I really like is the beautiful variations of color and the variety in the headdresses and how it matches their clothes. I think it is so exotic. I think they are so disciplined.

If this statement were made during a group discussion with students, you would want to avoid having the conversation shift toward simple sharing of various admirations. Again, focus on the feelings provoking the statement from the student. You might want to acknowledge the strength it took for the student to own and say out loud to the group that she did not know about the history and meaning behind wearing a hijab. You may want to reassure the group that it is normal to feel anxious about the unknown. As the facilitator, you may want to introduce resources to the group that would help them learn more about Muslims of various races. Focus on exploring the complexities of racism and religious privilege that are underlying her statement. You might ask the students to explore in depth what she means by *disciplined,* and contrast that with her assumptions about Christian religions. You may want to explore the many messages sent about skin color and appearance in this society. And ask the group to explore the expectations of what is normal and beautiful. As a facilitator, your goal would be to have the participants explore feelings about the complexity of the issue related to religion and race and shift the focus away from surface-level observations.

Benevolence Potential Responses. A benevolence defensive response is based on displaying an overly sensitive attitude toward a social and political issue based on an attitude of charity. The millennial generation of college students is said to be demographically the most diverse group of college students (Broido, 2004). In addition, many have studied abroad or participated in service-learning projects that have boosted their feelings of confidence about their ability to face diversity issues. And yet while millennial students attending college today may have been exposed to more diversity, they likely have not thoroughly explored issues related to power, privilege, and oppression in depth or "what it means to function honorably in a multicultural community" (Watt, 2007, p. 114). When challenged to explore in more depth the role of religion, privilege, and service in one's life, a student may respond:

I have participated in service-learning trips over spring break to help members of communities who are ill, disabled, or have suffered some type of devastation. Last year, I did missionary work in war-torn countries where I brought the message of democracy. Each time I have felt overwhelmed by the feelings of support and gratitude expressed by those receiving the help. I know that injustice exists, but I feel that if I keep helping those who are less fortunate than I, then I am making a difference.

In general, focus on the assets the students bring and compliment them on their commitment to service. As a facilitator, you would have to encourage the students to explore the dynamics of power and privilege that are in acts of charity. You could do this by asking them to consider how acts of charity are centered on both the power of the giver and the powerlessness of the target population. You might ask the group to consider how reaching down to help those less fortunate than yourself can contribute to maintaining the current dominant society structure. Ask the student to grapple with the question: "What am I getting from this interaction?" Your goal as a facilitator is to guide participants to explore their emotionally intense feelings about the intersections of religious privilege along with ableism or classism and not allow them to avoid the discomfort by focusing on their goodwill.

Privileged Identity Exploration (PIE) Model: Relevant Applications of Foundational Principles. In sum, the foundation of the PIE model suggests that responses such as the ones exemplified above are primal responses born out of feelings of fear or entitlement, or both. The fear in the case of religious privilege might be based in the threat the questioning of shared values and beliefs brings to social relationships, especially familial. The need to respond defensively could also be rooted in an entitled attitude reinforced by the societal insulation of Christian or religious privilege that exists in American culture. As a facilitator, it is useful to understand the source of these defenses because it will help you to empathize with students and yet keep focused on the goal of raising their critical consciousness.

Suggestions for Creating Conditions for Productive Difficult Dialogues

Why is it important to encourage dialogue about the intersections of religious privilege? It is important for student affairs practitioners to find ways to effectively manage dialogues at the intersections of religious privilege on college campuses in America. Nash, Bradley, and Chickering (2008) point out three concerns of sixteen college presidents: (1) an increase in a polarizing tone in academic debate that silences controversial views, (2) a proliferation of threats toward academic freedom and a rise in anti-Semitic, anti-Muslim, and anti-Arab incidents, and (3) a lack of responsibility for constructive dialogue that is carried by all higher education administrators rather than just student affairs professionals. A call is out to institutions of higher education to find more ways to have constructive difficult dialogue facilitated by faculty, academic administrators, and student affairs professionals on campus (Nash, Bradley, and Chickering, 2008). Here are three conditions to help create the emotional and intellectual space for difficult dialogues:

- *Acknowledge the dominant and marginalized paradigm.* Realize that the concerns of many individuals from marginalized groups are at least in part related to systemic and external forces rather than internal psychological problems or deficiencies. There are subtle ways that the dominant system is upheld and reinforced in dialogue. By simply not intentionally acknowledging the dominant and marginalized paradigm, a facilitator can reinforce the dominant societal structure. Therefore, as a facilitator, you have to overtly and in conscious ways acknowledge dominance in language and practices. For example, be conscious of the use of pronouns, such as referring to the dominant group (Christians) as "us" and mainstream and the marginalized group (atheists) as "them" or not mainstream. Find ways to equalize the view of the dominant and marginalized groups in the dialogue by referring to both groups objectively as belief systems, thereby taking away the feeling of ownership and the power inherent in the silent assumptions that one group holds the prevailing interest of society.

- *Understand the personal and social investment.* Recognize that discussions about religious privilege are central to identity (Jones and McEwen, 2000). Avoid approaching dialogue in ways that are punitive; instead, communicate an understanding that these issues are deeply connected to family and traditions that comprise our personal and social identities. Affirm their emotion. Acknowledge that it is difficult to engage in discussions about religion, and yet reinforce that college is a place for facing challenging questions, exploring ideas, and developing identity.

- *Tap the potential power in paradox.* View paradox and polarities as opportunities for dialogue and deeper reflection rather than problems to solve (Johnson, 1996). As a facilitator, treat the tension around disagreement and the resulting uncomfortable feelings as normal and appropriate. Allow students the space to examine their beliefs and contradicting ideas. Focus on the process and the new awareness that comes forth when exploring the interdependent nature of paradoxes rather than on an end point of solving the problem. This can create an atmosphere that invites students to have the courage to boldly face ideals that challenge their belief system.

Using these three conditions will help to create environments where students feel freer to examine contradictory belief systems and develop their identity. More important, students who have been traditionally marginalized (Jews, Muslims, and atheists) on campuses and excluded because of the dominant social structure associated with religious privilege will be included by allowing a more complex conversation about beliefs that goes beyond discussions of good and bad or right or wrong and more directly address the multifaceted advantages within the social system.

Conclusion

It is important for student affairs professionals to create opportunities for students to engage in difficult dialogues about religious privilege. Developing the skills and experience to facilitate these dialogues is equally important. Using frameworks such as the PIE model can help student affairs professionals who are facilitating these difficult dialogues by identifying behaviors that often derail productive conversation and employing strategies to help focus the discussions on issues that will help to increase students' critical consciousness. As a wise colleague said to me, "It is the paradox that brings the leader forth" (F. O. Matthews, personal communication, April 18, 2008). Paradox is inherent in discussions about religious privilege, and teaching students skills to grapple with polarities by simultaneously holding the tension of opposites will ultimately make them better leaders in our society.

References

Broido, E. M. "Understanding Diversity in Millennial Students." In M. D. Coomes and R. Debard (eds.), *Serving the Millennial Generation.* New Directions in Student Services, no. 106. San Francisco: Jossey-Bass, 2004.

Freire, P. *Pedagogy of the Oppressed.* New York: Continuum, 1970.

Fried, J. "Thinking Skillfully and Respecting Difference: Understanding Religious Privilege on Campus." *Journal of College and Character,* 2007, *9*(1), 1–7.

Goodman, D. J. *Promoting Diversity and Social Justice: Educating People from Privileged Groups.* Thousand Oaks, Calif.: Sage, 2001.

Johnson, B. *Polarity Management: Identifying and Managing Unsolvable Problems.* Amherst, Mass.: HRD Press, 1996.

Jones, S. R., and McEwen, M. K. (2000). "A Conceptual Model of Multiple Identity Development." *Journal of College Student Development,* 2000, *41*(4), 405–414.

Logan, C. R. "Homophobia? No, Homoprejudice." *Journal of Homosexuality,* 1996, *31*(3), 31–53.

Nash, R. J., Bradley, D. L., and Chickering, A. W. *How to Talk About Hot Topics on Campus: From Polarization to Moral Conversation.* San Francisco: Jossey-Bass, 2008.

Reason, R. D, and Davis, T. L. "Antecedents, Precursors, and Concurrent Concepts in the Development of Social Justice Attitudes and Actions." In R. D. Reason, N. Evans, E. Brodio, and T. L. Davis (eds.), *Developing Social Justice Allies.* New Directions in Student Services, no. 110. San Francisco: Jossey-Bass, 2005.

Seifert, T. "Understanding Christian Privilege: Managing the Tensions of Spiritual Plurality." *About Campus,* May-June 2007, pp. 10–17.

Watt, S. K. "Difficult Dialogues, Privilege and Social Justice: Uses of the Privileged Identity Exploration (PIE) Model in Student Affairs Practice." *College Student Affairs Journal,* 2007, *26*(2), 114–126.

SHERRY K. WATT *is an associate professor in Graduate Programs in Student Affairs in the Division of Counseling, Rehabilitation, and Student Development, University of Iowa.*

INDEX

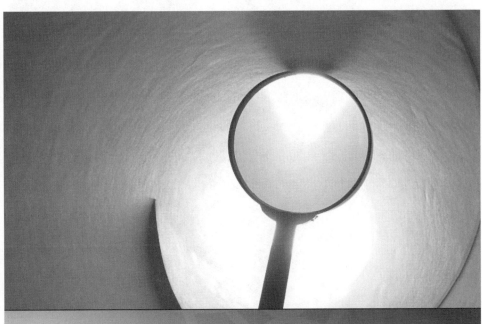

Why Wait to Make Great Discoveries

When you can make them in an instant with Wiley InterScience® Pay-Per-View and ArticleSelect™

Now you can have instant, full-text access to an extensive collection of journal articles or book chapters available on Wiley InterScience. With Pay-Per-View and ArticleSelect™, there's no limit to what you can discover...

ArticleSelect™ is a token-based service, providing access to full-text content from non-subscribed journals to existing institutional customers (EAL and BAL)

Pay-per-view is available to any user, regardless of whether they hold a subscription with Wiley InterScience.

Benefits:

• Access online full-text content from journals and books that are outside your current library holdings
• Use it at home, on the road, from anywhere at any time
• Build an archive of articles and chapters targeted for your unique research needs
• Take advantage of our free profiled alerting service the perfect companion to help you find specific articles in your field as soon as they're published
• Get what you need instantly no waiting for document delivery
• Fast, easy, and secure online credit card processing for pay-per-view downloads
• Special, cost-savings for EAL customers: whenever a customer spends tokens on a title equaling 115% of its subscription price, the customer is auto-subscribed for the year
• Access is instant and available for 24 hours

⊕WILEY
InterScience®
DISCOVER SOMETHING GREAT

www.interscience.wiley.com

Photography: Pawel Rosolek

4760b